New and Selected Poems, 1962–92

New and Selected Poems, 1962–92

LAURENCE LIEBERMAN

9/25/92

For Jim,

with best wishes,

Larry

UNIVERSITY OF ILLINOIS PRESS

Urbana and Chicago

© 1993 by Laurence Lieberman
Manufactured in the United States of America
1 2 3 4 5 C P 5 4 3 2 1

This book is printed on acid-free paper.

Library of Congress Cataloging-in-Publication Data
Lieberman, Laurence.
  [Poems. Selections]
  New and selected poems, 1962–92 / Laurence Lieberman.
    p.   cm.
  ISBN 0-252-02010-3 (cl). — ISBN 0-252-06314-7 (pb)
  I. Title.
PS3562.I43N48   1993
 811'.54—dc20   92-45567
                                                    CIP

Acknowledgments

The author gratefully acknowledges the editors of the following journals, in which these poems first appeared.

The American Poetry Review: "Psychodrama: Tokyo Mime Film," "The Tilemaker's Hill Fresco," "Eros at the World Kite Pageant," "Moonlighters," "The Organist's Black Carnation," "The Banana Madonna," "The Mural of Wakeful Sleep," "The Skateboard Throne: An Ode to Citizen Amputees," "The Creole Mephistopheles"

The Atlantic Monthly: "My Father Dreams of Baseball"

Boulevard: "Prayer Against the Curse Bomb"

Carleton Miscellany: "Black Lotus of the Links," "The Spearing," "Homage to Austin Warren"

The Carrell: "Girard, Girard," "82 × 48"

The Chariton Review: "Tartine, for All Her Bulk," "Tartine, Strumming Her Opera"

The Hudson Review: "Santana," "Tarpon," "Flying Below Sea Level," "Skin-Flying into the Storm Center," "Island Trashfires," "Flamingos of the Soda Lakes," "Queen of the Billiards," "Courtship of the Jersey Lineman"

The Kenyon Review: "The Dungeon Amorist," "Swimming Pool Pastoral"

The Nation: "Saltcod Red," "The Banana Dwarf," "Siesta"

New England Review: "Loves of the Peacocks," "Bulwark"

The New Yorker: "The Family Tree," "The Unblinding," "Transvestite," "The Osprey Suicides," "Kimono," "God's Measurements," "Nara Park: Twilight Deer Feeding"

The Paris Review: "Corners"

Partisan Review: "The Kofukuji Arsonists"

Poetry: "The House Skin," "Skin Song," "Lobsters in the Brain Coral," "Daibutsu"

Quarterly Review of Literature: "Increasing Night," "Love, the Barber"

The Reaper: "Sunday: My Throat Afire"

The Saturday Review: "Inside the Gyroscope"

Sewanee Review: "Wreckage of the Pagoda Moons," "Woman's Tongue"

Southern Review: "Stubby Carrot"

Southwest Review: "Tartine's Banishment"

The Yale Review: "The Coral Reef," "The Diving Ballet," "Song of the Thrush"

Special thanks to the National Endowment for the Arts and to the Center for Advanced Study of the University of Illinois for Creative Writing Fellowships, which supported the completion of poems in this book.

for Binnie

Contents

New Poems

Courtship of the Jersey Lineman

Stan and
Monica. Monica and Stan. Met last year
in Jersey
at shoulder-heave battering ram. She scored highest, wielding
the heavy steel mallet. Monica kept slamming the Muscle-
man bell at the top
of the tower of sputtering white lights lined-up in a row.
A trick snap of her wrists?
No mere fluky swing! She rang the topmost bell three times in quick

succession.
He struck the respectable He-Man level,
two full notches
below *her* Hercules pinnacle . . . Secretly, she loved the way
he curled his upper lip in a pout—a man who lost, often,
yet never felt whipped.
But oh he was menaced, *wasted,* from the moment he set eyes
on the purple butterfly
tattoo, wholly visible, exposed on her thigh, blooming just under

the crossed
ties of her bikini shorts . . . Stan—back home
in Passaic—
is a lineman who straps iron crampons to his shoe bottoms
and carries electric meters on a sling around his neck
when he shinnies up poles
to run routine checks, or repair hitches in wires and cables
that feed power to the trains—
both subway and elevated . . . Often, after dates, Monica tagged along.

Night shifts,
she kidded with him on homemade walkie-talkies,
while he spooled out
the fresh coils of wire, re-working many a faulty circuit.

So went the drift of their shy slow courtship. They anatomized
        shifting wind directions, howls
altered to whistling, the steady whine of taut wires in hard gales,
        the crackle of slack wires in gusts.
One or the other would warn the radar-mate of sudden belly wallops,

        hard blows due
    to arrive in six to eight seconds of their stop-
        watches' slow dials.
    She might walk ahead a quarter mile, a half mile, and report
weather conditions back to him down the line, ten or twenty
        high power poles behind.
They played so earnestly at relaying the weather crisis bulletins—
        divulged with such exact scrutiny
of details—he often forgot it was a private game they'd improvised.

        His safety,
    perched on the upper pole ladder rungs, depended—
        wholly—on her air
current accounts, her accurate samplings of moisture levels
and shifting forms of precip—rain, sleet, hail, snow, duststorm,
        or freezing rain—each variant
posing a different hazard to the lineman; and she marveled
        at the exquisite fine shadings
in his tactile sense, his dexterity with hairsbreadth twists and twines

        of wire-ends;
    while she dreaded the risks of sparking, outage,
        short circuit,
    overheating and burnout, or actual flash fires on the line.
Despite his huge puffy asbestos insulated gloves, he knew
        the touch of every line quirk,
eyes averted . . . The days she stayed home sick, or indolent,

he felt deserted. None of his tools
worked right: the shears' edge dulled, the soldering iron stayed cold,

the nail heads
always crumpled too soon, leaving the nails
half-in, half-out
of the power poles . . . When they'd met at the hammer-slugger's stall
at the County Fair, the play grew serious at once, a work of love
between them. Blows of the steel
hammer head sparked an electric shining of skin-tingling rush
between two unacknowledged opponents,
before either spoke a word. Now his work had turned up new forms of play

they shared.
She loved to work the coastal rocks near Passaic
Falls, and she climbed
ledges to inspect large bird nests in cliff-top eyries. She chose
the most unscalable shelves, or those which looked impassable
to her lineman, atop his pole
in the distance, who waved back to her in amazement at the surprise
pinnacle of each new feat of rock-
scrabbling, his binoculars at a loss to pick out any entryway, as if

she'd floated
the last twenty yards' ascent on wings of the chatter
which kept circulating
between their two sets of ear phones; she taking a true zeal
in finding higher roosts to mount than nearby public works towers,
or the railways' control towers
he had to monitor from topmost footrests. What an elation
she felt waving down to him! Or waving
back to the townspeople and schoolchildren, who greeted her with awe

and disbelief
(as they might an unfamiliarly plumaged new species
of gull) through windows
of trains speeding out of tunnel mouths. She felt like a flasher
when the train crowds ogled her, but never displayed the cobra
tattoo on her left buttock
to train-loads of passengers roaring past, though she'd often tease Stan
with threats of such masqueradery.
Which he pretended to ignore. But he leered at her in expectant shame

as trains drew
near to the unexpected sideshow she offered
to private first-class
car, economy coach, and diner, alike . . . They married. She'd
returned to her half-time job as ticket taker at the Fair,
and he missed her twin eagle
companionship on the job, the freedom they shared: he flying
from pole to pole wound in his coils
of ropes and cables; she scrabbling like a mountain goat in crannies,

cliff dugouts.
They were two high-flyers off the Jersey seacoast!
They spread their arms wide
from respective towers, to wave blessings, to keep their balance,
but wider, to embrace the day's happy expanse as great sea birds
soar on outspread wings for long
and long riding of the currents—these, too, rode out the rise and fall
of northwesterly wind currents,
rode out the laughter and technical data and witty repartee that passed

between them,
sizzled along the sparking wires of the two-way
radio receivers (capped
with short three-segmented antennae) they carried. Oh they rode out

the mounting waves of mutual desire in this rare aerial stilt-
        walking flirtation and courtship,
    beckoning to each other over bridges, across river channels, ditches,
        and waving flares, when other forms
of visual contact between them failed; his next moves always plotted

        in advance,
        mapped out by the company railroad's computer
            printout of key snags
    on the line needing emergency repairs. But *her* itinerary
of hikers' trails, daring zigzags, ascents and descents, followed
        an ever-changing impromptu
    pattern of swerves. She might pursue a course parallel to his job
        circuit—a mirror image, perhaps.
Or she might be prompted to follow her own pure whimsy and caprice.

        The radio
        contact that linked them was never interrupted,
            not even when he donned
    scuba-diving gear and performed delicate underwater rewirings,
    all equipment sealed airtight, waterproofed . . . But she couldn't bear
        to see him *fry* that day, his face
    lit with a charge that might have killed a man who had not, as had he,
        in eight years' service on the line,
built up immunity to electrocution, as some have innured their guts

        to huge doses
        of poison, by absorbing at least a dozen
            high voltage shocks
    on the job. He'd shown her the eyebrow permanently erased
by the livewire's instant deep-fry, the long scar taking a couple
        of snake loops around his wrist
    and forearm. One side or the other of the white double S-curve

could be taken for wounds of a knife-
fight, but the winding curves of the scar were telltale electric snake

        whiplash marks . . .
        Even so, she wasn't prepared for the exploding star
            of light which commenced
        as a tiny fireflysized bulb of yellow, and inflated. It grew—
    in one long second—into a dazzling sphere of phosphorescent gold,
            its aura surrounding his whole
        ladder-top figure bent over forward, starkly silhouetted
            in a grasshopper's crouch, arms curled
    over his head to ward off the blast! He vanished, utterly, from view

        for two seconds
        (longer, perhaps, the flash blinding to she who stared
            hard at the flaming core
        and did not flinch), as if his whole body mass disintegrated,
    churned into gold-leaf excelsior blossoms. She turned away,
            already catching the stench
    of his singed hair, burnt skin, braced to meet *death's face.* But he,
            making no sound, had belt-shinnied
    halfway down the pole, shaking his head and patting one side of his face

        like a swimmer
        flushing water from a plugged ear; then, he blinked
            again and again, each time
        harder: "No, I'm not in pain," he pleaded. "Not burnt bad.
    Not dying. These flashes happen. But I'm blinded worse this time.
            Can't seem to open my eyes atall."
    And the pops had deafened one ear . . . His eyes still stuck together,
            she led him home—whacking his bum ear
    with the heel of his palm. Next day, after five or six eyewash rinsings,

          sight returned,
       his ears still ringing, but not loud enough to drown
         her howls. He must quit
     his job! "No problem," he says. "Those loose-circuitry sparks
and blown transformer blasts are all bark, no bite. Knocks me out
        for a day or two, at the outside."
Open-handed, she boxed him on *both* ears, and wept—then fell, dead away,
     in a faint. And foreswore their engagement.
Back to the fairgrounds box office for her . . . Next week, they married.

Prayer Against the Curse Bomb

Last month, two years to a day since Dave Shaw's
    house burned down,
        just before dusk and day's last light crumpled,
          a soft gray purselike missile
        shot through his frontroom window, landing at his feet
with a gentle thud. It seemed to weigh no more

          than a dead gull's
        carcass: *unwinged, nonfeathered, but a birdbreasted shape.*
He ran to the open window
    hunting a glimpse—however fleeting—
        of the messenger, but no sign. That lumpy bulb, below,
    had been flung with hairline
accuracy, dead center, through his third story
        window—perhaps hurled from a sling, or fired by blowgun

    across the distance. Gingerly, he lifted
        the leather pouch,
          suede-soft, velvety, as if it might explode
            when handled roughly, noticed
        that it was sewn shut from the inside, the worst kind
of ill omen! Looked again, still no deliverer

          anyplace in sight.
        His throat constricted, and soon he was fighting for breath.
He could not fake himself out;
    after a lifelong tutelage in science,
        trained naturalist that he was, this he knew for fact—
yes, supernatural fact,
a pouch sewn from within, all threads concealed,
        hid from view, from touch, contains *one thing* or *the other.*

There are exactly two ways about it,
    not one, not three.

Either it is a grueling heavy curse
    upon the finder, finder's
      home and family; or it's a blessing. Only a trained
   shaman, at best a Haitian necromancer,

        is fit to decipher
      the contents of the packet, whether accursed or beneficent.
If the latter, the trinkets,
   stones, jewels, foul-smelling animal
      remains or straw shreds placed therein, however meager
  or inconsequent they appear,
could be stored for protection against the most pungent
      furies, or demons, in the years ahead. Now a full-certified

Black Magic cabalist must be summoned
    at once, perhaps
      imported by urgent plea from neighbor
        isles—Saba or St. Kitts—
      if no local maestro can be found promptly. But word
  of the present calamity soon drew forth

        a visitor guru
      from Guadeloupe, who came toting a small wooden barrel
on his back (chained and padlocked shut),
   which contained his wiremesh and rubberized
      tinwork paraphernalia; this box perhaps an Occultist
  version of police bomb squad's
tool bin of electronics gear scaled for defusing
      a live bomb, *or dud.* Mr. Griffin, at first eye contact,

spotted the insewn leatherette as genuine,
   the real thing,
      he'd bet his life on it. *The identification*
        be never in doubt, he warned

David. Sagacity dripped from his brow, in the form
of a true light sweat, as if he feared *de curse*

    bomb, without delay,
  might be triggered before he neutralized its contents,
catching him, along with intended
  victim, in *de crossfire of conflagration.*
  And now he must know, to the exact square centimeter,
  which patch of cedar hardwood
floor was first touched by the soft packet. Just so.
  A V-shaped grain in the wood, David recalls, like wishbone-

of-chicken arch. Here the leading corner
  struck. Bag took
    one hop, three or four inches, then slid
      a meter or so. Grif draws
    a wide chalk circle around the point of first impact,
  perhaps five feet in diameter. He stands

    in this circle's
  center for some moments, mumbles inaudibly with his lips,
fingers tapping forehead, while silent
  numerical computations—O magic numbers!—
  seem to fill the air before he speaks. *Monsieur Shaw,*
  you must fetch seven dollars
and eleven cents, to de penny, exact change, plus
  a full unopened bottle of rare aged rum, though de brand

be hard to come by in zeeze parts, distilled
  in old Hayti.
    No imitation or substitute will soo-fyze . . .
    He falls into a deep trance,
    eyes staring inward, no other sound escapes his throat,
  his breathing slows, lulls, seems to stop.

David races here
and there about town, locating first the prescribed rum,
dollars, one dime, but that lone copper
penny gives him most trouble. He returns
to the walkup flat, catches Grif rummaging in his kit—
who ferrets out, at last,
six other ingredients: powders, incense
sticks, tinctures, bug parts . . . Commenceth the Exorcism!

With great flourish of arm twists, Grif opens
squat miniature
rum flask, rotating bottle around corkscrew
held steady over his head;
blindly, he mutters a few latinate oaths, and sucks
one great puffcheeked mouthful of spirits, stays

bloated two minutes
staring popeyed, then releases his fat balloon of face
with a sneeze burst of spray, rum mists
and droplets squirted in all directions
suffusing the air about his head—*we vanquish all*
de evil wraiths dat hover
near, snuff zem out right quick! The next moment,
he pours a precise half-moon arc of rum, just filling

the anterior chalk semicircle that encloses
their shoes, David
now stationed on tiptoe behind mentor Grif,
who—with wizardly gusto—
lights one long wooden matchstick on his scratchy cap
visor, and sets the rum floor patch ablaze,

tall flames shooting
up to their chins, so hot they scorch David's close-trimmed

beard. And then, with one backhanded swing
  of his machete, Grif flicks out the whole curved
    pool of fire: POOF!, quenched so fast you couldn't know
  he'd lifted the blade yet.
It's done, says he. *Duh demons of de pouch*
  are moshed, choked into de void. Dey flies away on tongues

  of de snuffed flame, no way for zem to escape
    de fire's attraction
      nor de fire's blowout! All's finish . . . He passes
        David a small paring knife
      drawn from his kit barrel, skull-and-crossbones carved
  on the ivory handle, and Grif commands him

          to fearlessly slice
        open the leather case, cutting along the seamless margin
chary to leave the contents unfrayed,
  intact. With hand shakes and moans, he cuts.
    Harmless wood shavings, herb roots and vines, pop out.
  False alarm! exclaims Grif,
angst mixed with relief. *Save zem good charms: ONE UP*
  on vermin. You makes de first move, if dey threats you . . .

Tartine, for All Her Bulk

Tartine, for all
her bulk outsweep—pumpkin hips
    and rump—pivots and revolves with burly grace
    across the several acres
    of yard, dashing from one garden corner to the next

        amid the gush
        of wit and loquacious repartee with Thom and myself.
Two donkeys and one calf,
    on separate ropes, get tangled
        in the pair of hoses, strategically set, placed
    to hit most key targets
of her sprawled vegetable and fruit gardens
        evenly: the calf keeps trying to munch the colorful

    leafage from young papaya and christophene
        plants, her prize crops,
            while a burro starts zigzagging, his rope
            crisscrossing the hoses,
            so we can hardly tell where any rope, hose or thick
        vine starts or stops. But she unravels

the loose flux
of knots, saves the tender shoots
    and battens down all free-floating livestock
    like so many sails or tarps
    in a gale at sea, with no loss of her verbal pizzazz.

        Steepest grades
        of garden, here and there, must be traversed if she's
to keep one jump ahead
    of the hemp and rubber entanglements,
        those hooved prancers grooved to outwit her, to do
    her one better—they lose!

She wields her fulsome girth, brawny and agile
       to spare, over those abrupt dips and ascents, perhaps two

   house stories' elevation at the loftiest
     plateau, where one hose—
        propped on a forked limb—splits its geyser
          into three or four streams
        aimed toward lowest fringes of her many crops. My eye
     cannot discern the measure of her amplest

haunch or loin,
what with ballooning skirts,
   pleated ruffles billowing in and out—
   those immensities veiled
   as she whirls about her gardens. She waves her lavish

          satin-gilt hems
        with a gypsy dancer's flourish, parading her costume
     flash with as much deviltry
        as the carriage she half conceals, half
          divulges: *oversize clothes,* she croons (picking up
        my gasps and dazzlement
     at the vervy sashaying of her skirt flounces),
        have frequently been a sideline and avocation of hers . . .

   In Britain, she'd traveled for some years
     as saleslady clothier
        and agent, modeling—from door to door—
          those prodigious garments
        she offered at slashed warehouse prices to corpulent
     sad-faced buyers. Tartine made a *Royal Killing*

of her walkup/
walkaway business, soonest won

top honors for best sales on her twenty-square-
miles route, three years running.
She kept the most capacious outsize smocks and slacks,

          pleated cape
       jackets and horsy riding britches, in *High Fashion*
by adorning their inflated
    hulks with her rotund—but agile—charms.
        Chunky allure, she terms it. Wherever she sojourned
on holiday, she could garner
quick pin money by peddling a ready-to-wear
    stack of eye-fetching ruffly blouses, or expansive gowns.

    Oddshaped folks, in City or Province,
        often too submissive
           and shy about their disproportioned limbs
              to shop in the marketplace,
           thus paying dear prices to local seamstress or tailor
for radical alterations of drab fabrics,

jumped at the chance
to embrace puffy shapes and offbeat
    sizes on their very doorstoop, while Tartine
    endowed many an article
    she wore with raw earthy glamours into the bargain,

        her sales pitch
           the Latin dance trot she varied to make each outfit
shine forth with proper flare.
    None haggled over price, so cheered
        they were to be lifted from a hopeless morass: hunts
    to clothes marts that catered,
only, to midrange norms . . . Today, since her return
        to Montserrat in nineteen eighty, she can hardly find

true fit duds for herself, much less a sales
    career which pays
        half so well—hard pressed for Overseas Mail
            Order garb from America
        or Britain: *I can't be sewin' up tentsized parachutes
        for me own glum bloody stay-at-home backside!*

Tartine's Banishment

When Tartine turned 20, her Papa
gave her a gorgeous red velvet tall hat—topped by an ostrich
    feather stretching overhead like a smokestack:
        she blubbered her thanks,
but trembled, a scared premonition . . . Next day,

    he shipped her to Britain (yoked
to sister and two cousins), to beg work: no jobs in Montserrat,
    too many mouths to feed at home, her dozen
        younger sibs. Two hours
notice! Just time enough to pack, her blood-colored

    flamy hat her one calling card.
She knew herself banished, a citizen deported from homeland
    and family: "My last word to pa   as I cross
        de thin gangplank: *I know*
I'll be daid in one week   Sink or swim   smiles he . . .

    Not so cruel   my boatswain Sire
He knows me for tough   Believe me, pard, in six fortnights
    more than half our boatload of Montserattians
        die   or fall to bum
thieving, prison   We fewer push on   For me,

    it was total chaos   Strange land
Most folks never saw my color   they be bug-eyed, staring
    me up and down and over   My fist pound doors
        of too many bottom wage
job employment offices to count   My first boss

    for part time clerking   be takin'
a fancy to me   sends me to six-week school program   I pass
    with High Honors   step into my Royal Blue

Uniform   Ensign cap'd do
my seagoing pa proud   if he could but see me

(No way to take snapshot   back dot
time   or he'd see)   I'se be first blackwoman Omnibus driver
   in Yorkshire Parish   O, much I could tell thee
      about poor Blacks' survival
in de Allwhite World   I don't see one other

   Black face in dat whole small
town   Everybody glarin' at me like I come over de Zoo fence
   A cross between a Cheetah and a Chimp   (No Sir,
      I wasn't melon-girthed
yet)   But dey take all de seats in my tramcar

   Best driver on de line, many say
So I cope eleven months   Cope, but I craves other Dark Souls
   One day I trip to London   few extra pounds
      saved out from four pounds
per week salary   two pounds for barebones lodging

   One pound for transport to work
No justice, you see   I profesh-nul driver, why no free fares?
   I pays thru de teeth   just for comings & goings
      Leaves one quid per week
for everything else   But I mail one shilling home

   each month   for family support
I hitcht ride to London, like I say, on my twenty-first birthday
   Phone home   Bawl and bawl to Pa: *please take
      me back   No way,* say he
Tartine luv bunny   you must stay three more year

at least, or 'til Montserrat jobs
be not so scarce   Howl my heart out   Take school for London
     subway work one month   Soon I be directing
          folks to make connexions
between a hundred trains underground   No room

     for mistakes, or people come back
angry   vengeful to tell you—you fouled dem up   sent dem
     down a blind alley   Now you say, *Sorry Bub,*
          beggin' ya pardon, pliz
Or you make it up to folks, someways   You stuck

     in de stall   between turnstiles
like a sitting duck   no way out   you gots to listen gots
     to just take it   So I cope   Always, de last
          attendant's mistakes keep
backfiring on me   But nobody payin' much mind

     to who it is gave 'em wrong tip
or wrong turn   Dey just wantin' Black Face to pin blame on
     From bus above to train below   de same panic
          and hustle, believe me . . .
Many a time, I thought I'd wear a bag over my head."

Tartine, Strumming Her Opera

Years back, I hitched to Jamaica husband   He makin' good

salary   One night, he surprise me with thick wad
of money—*buy yourself gift*
say he   *You needs new dress, to look*
'spectable at work
But halfway to lady's Boutique

I spot guitar in band supply window   my heart, lump

in my throat, she melt
and I blow all my dress wampum
on de box and strings
My Kingston Man   he trow big fit!   Neck veins
swell   forehead bulge   like man having dope seizure

Never again, he give me quid   earned scooping de clutter

from streets before daybreak   to buy myself TOY
when he say frilly dress   tidy duds
be what I most needs
Fine wit me   say I, *I rather*
make music 'stead of be clotheshorse

(But I knows he right to be sore)   For two weeks I practice

pulling de string   every spare minute I snatch
between turnstile meter maid chores
token handouts   When I knows
I'se ready, I punch
time clock for shift end   I flies

I goes down to train underground   directly below my dayshift

subway work stall   Now I sees
de Musicmakers—wooing foot traffic passers-by
wit der sweet sounds   takin' turns, polite & orderly
One tall man hangin' back   he merely jingles
short string of bells

from bent hand & hums   flute   piccolo   harmonica   fiddle

Each one be drawin' a little circle
of fans around he   So I bust onto dat scene
hoistin' my guitar
I offers to play most ANY TUNE
Plenty folks take me up on it   But my patrons jeer

and stomp, when I miss half de notes   on my first few gigs

Many music lovers forgive my bum memory
Soon we laughin' and jokin' about it   *need no apology,*
say they   I pleads and begs
dem, one by one   *hum yo' FAV–O–RIT A–RI–A*
I calls de choiring OPERA

or OPERETTA   no matter how far offkey dey wails an' screech

We all be forgivin' each other's mistakes   so fast
it's like a bloody contest
between us   to be de better sport
I learns de melody   regardless
how hoarse   or rattly   or gravel-throated

be my Sing Coach   by night end, I getting all de tunes right

First one string   den all six
I offers to pay folks

for partnerin' my tuneups   but de chums always flip
few coins   or crinkled paper quid
notes   into my upturned cap

Willock, 82   my pal Thomas
Just 48   12 offspring apiece: it's a joyous sport
   High rivalry between them   or numbers game
They play, when they get revved up

   Tongues rotary engines, flywheels
Awhirl in their throats   If you break into their parley
   In mid fracas, you might take the odds   stats
Quotas   bandied to and fro

   For bets on Racehorse   high stakes
Tabs in the Carib Lotteries   they come in at Dead Heat
   Contest tied-up, in sheer numbers of kids
Scant 12 each   so let's get down

   To cases   numbers in versus out
Of Wedlock buys short shrift   meer tally of Breeder
   Moms uncounted   But these two Jakes do stay
Accountable   to all past loves

   Past offspring   floating some gifts
Some food & rent assist   or flat money handouts: point
   Of Honor   child support a Sacred Given
In their ranks   no talk of alimony

   Palimony   or court fines   O who
Can deny siring babes   when so much pride   tall repute
   Accrues to each stud's boastful tot Head
Count . . . Our banter drifts to feats

   Of record fathering   career peaks
Pitched to charm my ear: Willock's two early sons born
   Thirty minutes apart, by two separate Moms
Beds in opposite corners   diagonal

Of the One   narrow Maternity Ward
Head Nurse   more boxing ref than Midwife   her hands full
    For trying to keep the two gals   Warriors
In separate cubicles   prior to last

    Hour, or so, of Labor   Each sprints
Three or four mad dashes   by turns   across the Ward
    Wielding fingernail scythes   Grim Reapers
To slash   that Other's eyes out

    Twin rage   simmering down in final
Minutes   to a Birthing Race   all that battle gusto
    Coupling with pelvic spasms   a Jousting
For scores   on Willock's point

    System   first one boy, then the other
Papa ecstatic   Declares the two males   equal winners
    Less than a half hour   between their First
Breaths   first allout squalls

    Of healthy furor . . . *I planned it thus,*
Winks Willock   *saved myself two trips to de hospital*
    Polished off both Nativity Vigils   and cork
Popper fests in de same hour   Houzzat

Stubby Carrot

Motor idling, we warble our greetings to nine roadside
squatters: two leaning on upright post, a few seated
on horizontal gate bars, the nearest stooped forward,

        rocking to and fro
     on his heels. A vague hushed
     camaraderie prevails—*hangin' out, hangin'*
tough, as a full-time
  avocation. At loose ends,
    all out of work, permanent layoffs,
    all retirees
and *ree-tahds* (do they get apt pensions, or endure
the homeless bread scarce pinch?) . . . One lame Nonagenarian.
    Two or three Octos,
     I'd wager. Longevities do abound, here,
   whatever the health

care void, care lapses. Balance of the crew, young chaps
who bear the look or stamp of handicap, a rheumyeyed drift—
if we seek nobility or grandeur in ranks of the disabled

      or feeble oldies,
    no such grace accrues here,
     broken spirits, all, if propped up a tad
by the league of lameness.
  I knows every Montserattian
    from de groun' up, murmurs Thomas,
    and howdy-dos
them, one by one, chanting snatches of each sad life
story—a bit overmuch like clever zookeeper, guide and zealot
     animal trainer,
      passing each cage, in turn, and rattling
   off choice tidbits

of the prize specimens' case histories, prior to capture.
Take Jocko. One eye poked out, oddly grayish socket exposed—
no patch. And arm permanently twisted back, hand purplish

           & shrunk. Both results
    of sole careless accident,
     while our Jocko worked as volunteer fireman,
the rural firehouse crew
  ever understaffed, bankrupt.
    Young Maylick, befogged and stone deaf
    since the gas main
exploded—while he patched leaky pipes, his assistant
forgot to unswitch the gas outlet (who, engulfed in fireball,
     fried to white ash
     in seconds). Mute Felix, whose tongue froze
  stuck during rescue

attempt: three kids swept downstream in heavy currents
of flashflood—a robust swimmer, he yelled his lungs hoarse
but couldn't bring himself to leap from shore to pursue

       the nursery school's
    ragdoll two-year-olds: babes
    atwirl like pinwheels, sucked under so quick
no one had time to blink.
  Just for one sec's failure
    of nerve, he'll never forgive himself—
    yet he forgets
how it all began, blindsided his memory: keeps trying
to talk to us, to explain how it is, but no way can he admit
    his recent muteness.
    Splut-splut. You have to dodge his spray
  as he gets worked up,

his neck veins bulging; he gags on his foamy scud, throat
billowing in and out with the effort . . . Thomas, undeterred,
recites the scalding flaws, face to face with each victim:

          some anonymous vague
      third party might be the butt
      of each grisly joke of Fate, while together
they whinny and squeal
    with pained hilarity to recount
      the single moment that severed this one's
      optic nerve,
frayed that one's spinal cord. *Shake han' with Gilmore*
(*I say!—de good left han', not dangled right claw*), who pays
      and pays every day
      of his ruined *Prime-O-Life* for ignoring
Thomas' good advice

ten years ago, this very week, when he was Gilly's foreman
at Shamrock Leaf Cable & Electric Co.: *Now dasn't thee turn
ever thy back on thy work, but always be keepin' thine eyes*

      fast t'where thee place
    thine limbs . . . But no, sad to say,
      our Gilly turned his back, the easier to raise
huge load, while his partner—
    who kept his eyes on the task,
      at least—stumbled on a crack in the road
      and dropt his end,
Gilly catching a full two-hundred-pounds' deadweight brunt
on two fingers. Thomas ran, fetched three sturdy crew to lift,
      all four together,
      so gently, that hefty block from thumb
    and back-bent forefinger,

one man perched at each corner of the wide steel armature;
but no use, the hand torn beyond repair, his index finger
rigid ever since, despite surgeon's patchup. *No fun i'tiz,*

> *Gilly can tell you, Sir,*
> *to hab dat one jointless*
> *stiff finger be pokin' outwards all duh while*
> *when you walks, talks, eats,*
> *be makin' good sex, or sleeps.*
> *It's like de one durn stubby carrot*
> *dat always pokes*
> *de hole through your sack when you returns from market*
> *and lets all de fruit & nuts be passin' through like a sieve*
> *before you notice*
> *de bag be growin' light on your shoulder—*
> *too late, all de food*

be lost (Gilly and Felix burst forth in wheezy snickers
and guffaws at Tom's proverbial trope): *de cats & goats*
hab snatched it up long pas' de time you spots duh leak!

Bulwark

Impossible, I'd have bet,
to drag the massive building units and materials
up this rugged crag's face: no access,
anyplace in view, for man traversals
over the rock-studded
hillslopes . . . Who can doubt the British took one hundred years,
or more, to build the *Brimstone Hill Fortress*
(close runner-up, for wizardly architectonics, to Christoph's
lofty *Citadel,*
cloud-nestled high above Haiti's Cap Haicien);
these steep cliff sweeps,
then, were proof against footfall or handhold
of clambering enemy troops,
piling ashore from ships anchored near this Gibraltar-
like protuberant small mountain,
seemingly as wide at the top as below,
a tall skull of earth
and rock, top-heavy with bulging cranium: a terrestrial
phrenologist would have a field day
measuring the skull's lofty bumps, from swelled cranial boulders
to wide jawbones . . .
And I'm weaving, jauntily, around the lower rim
of those jowls, today,
in my spiffy rental Toyota Starlet
on one lane winding upgrade,
signposts at every bend sporting red pictures
of goat or wide-bodied minibus,
by turns, above black letters BLOW HORN;
and though I depress
my dull horn constantly, a mad percussionist of fortress
jaw, my incessant beep-beeps are ignored
by all speedy downhill traffic and frequent wildlife meanderers
alike, stone deaf
to my wrist-weary honks and blorts, tire squeals

as well, as I dodge
many a passer. It is I, alone, who cling
            to the small shriveled patches
                of road edge, grassless, wheelrutted—downhill plungers
        always depending on *my* defensive swerves
                and parries, never giving way an inch
        or slowing their descent.
        By these sorties, I'm kept in mind of famed battles and sieges
                of these narrow all-but-impassable cliff
    lanes, revived in my survival tactics. Adjacent hillscape
grows oblique, ever
            steeper, when I nearly graze or sideswipe
            a twenty-foot-wide toothed
rampart, too near the road for safe auto leeway:
                its man-tall stone blocks unswayed,
                    wholly intact across three centuries despite thick roots
        and vines threading mossy cracks. I fancy
            a few small cannons or infantry muskets
        poked through the grooves
        between low turrets; and I try to fathom the daring needed
                by advancing French footsoldiers, sore taxed
    with finding traction to heel, claw and knuckle their way
    over bare rockface,
            so to scale the wickedly trackless and grooveless
            sandstone flanks. I scan
those colorveined and marbled slates, whether shale,
                granite, obsidian or marl
            I know not; but how can mere booted or sandaled hoofers,
        rope-tossing scouts, setting anchor for heft
            and lift—here and there—make headway, yes,
    against these incisor
    and fierce bicuspid ramparts, row by row of fanged bastions:
            numerous sets of teeth in the cliff's jaws,
    layered like rows of sharks' teeth, seemingly no end to the tiers

of fortress segments
     I pass, always positioned at surprise bends
     and wavy switchbacks—
tucked in the mountain's natural contours.
        Each parapet, as I ascend
        the hill's vast midsection, grows thicker, more awesome
    than the one before, and as I approach
       the fortress height, some few batteries
   raise two or three ranks
   of turreted cannon emplacements, one row earth-buttressed
      upon another's back: impregnable . . .
Often, I suppose I meet the great fort itself, but no, it's yet
another wing,
     layer, or level of patchwork bastion; so again,
     I conjure up memory
of the French forces who laid siege, those dogged
        relentless batterers who'd burst
       through these protective fortifications, many wall units
   so shrewdly wedded to the natural pitch
     and swing of cliff environs, they appear
  to be root-sprung
   outgrowths borne of the hill's deep crust, wide flat mushrooms
     of battery wall . . . At last, I am passing
through steel gates and meet the fully restored *Prince of Wales
Bastion*—commanding
    a vantage upon its wide esplanade of summit,
    one integral plateau
claimed to itself, crowning the bulwark skull.

FROM

The Unblinding

1968

The Family Tree

For Binnie

Unable to sleep,
he halts the river
of mindless thought
and starts to feel
the thoughts he wills.
The sounds of a house
asleep are stark,
remote. He tries
to listen for life,
to hear the walls
shake out their answers
to ultimate questions.

Is he carried
by his two feet
from room to room
before he pauses
to think to rise?
And seeing the moon
squander light
where no one sees
the fields his eyes
must look upon
with puzzled wonder,
will no voice come

to speak of loss
and fill the space
of his absent presence?
The tree in the yard
puts on new life.
A twisting juniper,

it turns in the night
and spirals upward.
Suddenly the tree
is in the room.
It feels no pain
but seems to shudder

with disbelief,
endued with warmth
held by the house.
The house presses
its life on the tree,
and swells to enclose
the life that fills it.
The man in the yard
puts down roots.
His legs are braced
in a stiff-kneed trance.
They mingle with earth.

As leaves of his hair
fall past his eyes,
the bush of his scalp
grows more full.
The shower of leaves
nearly smothers his breath
as he tries to step out
of his textured skin.
The tree in the house
motions to the man
as a thing blessed.
It gestures. He follows.

The two lock roots
below the foundations
and seal a pact
that lifts the house.
Wherever he looks
there are branches. Vines.
They circle his wife
as a delicate ivy,
and lace the bars
of his daughter's crib.
A family has risen.
The house vanishes.

The Unblinding

For my student, upon the anniversary
of the operation that restored his sight

When I think of my fear
of moving through my dreamed
life into the tough, unknown, real
images that burn my senses and mind
more fiercely than human
events that stick

in the craw of biographies,
when I shy away
from the incandescent moments that fall
into my hands unsought, un-
deservedly given or lent
to me, visions,

so to say, that can—and do
on occasion—sweep me off into their own
orbits, shattering my known self
into ill-fitting puzzle
pieces, and grinding
each fragment to smithereens,

leaving me numb to objects,
to the feel of a thing, to all identities
clogged, hopelessly blocked . . . I find
I try again, taught
by my student, Robert Beegle,
who was here today

leaning sail on a puff
of wind five thousand miles out from Cal-
ifornia to say hello   here

I am   fully bearded   one hundred years
younger than the eighteen-year-old
death-of-me you met

two years ago   Mr. Lieberman
And it is true. ←   1st sentence
He has grown younger more quickly
than anyone old I have
known. When I first
fastened my twenty-twenty two eyes on two

totally blinded at age
four in a traffic
mishap, two stillborn egg yolks
immobile in vacant
sockets, I saw a being sunk
within and drilling

deeper, as the innermost rings
in the trunk of a withered
sycamore, dying inward.
In the front row
next to the door (at his feet, the seeing-
eye German shepherd, head

on his paws, licking
and snuffling toward bell-time,
often mistaking a distant horn or whistle
for the hour-gong), the handicapped
listener shivered his lips
to decipher braille

that flew past shortwave
of fingertips,

the lips racing to overtake the fingers,
casting about within for broken
tape-ends of emotions
straggling from reels of earliest

childhood. I felt my eyes
clamber into hollowness, opening
in him like a bottomless
pit. Once exposed, it overflowed his face
and spread around the class,
like a skin

tightening. We could not breathe.
He shut his eyes.
Words failed—our voices
drawn into declivities of his nose
and mouth—
the room becoming an abyss

over which we teetered
dizzily. I looked and looked. Where
I had seen clearly
before grew blind spots
now. I saw too near,
too far, sight

locked. I had
to try not to see him,
to lay violent hands upon the light,
to make it bend
around his chair and twist
over his clenched,

sight-slaying face.
My skull bones grew
in weight,
converging on the delicate
flesh of eyeballs. Then, for days,
I walked shakily,

one foot stretched
before me, hunting anchorage (safe
lodging) like the tip of a white
cane, tapping . . . One morning, I glanced
about, dazedly—he stood
beside me, no one

I had ever seen before
outside his dog's
life, extending the pink absence slip
for my O.K. I saw (powerless
to believe) he saw my face,
smiling his first

look of me, the words
loosening from his tongue
as sparrows from a shaken clothesline.
One flick of a surgeon's knife
struck long-idle retinas
into perfect sight.

The House Skin

For James Dickey

In the clear night the hills
Do not deceive   they are desperately near   unwild
   Beasts cling to their sides   trustworthy
Horses   cows   goats   all

   In love with my children with yours
The gentle   (even the bulls, even the hornèd
   Heads)   The hills lean back to heads'
To-and-fro munching   the long

   Narrow horse-faces plunged
In milk-bowls of stars   pausing to lift their jaws
   Awash in moonlight dripping from whiskers,
The wide faces of cows

   Stretching leathery jowls their whale-
Tongues lapping galaxies   leaning at any angle to ravines
   To hillsides   in perfect balance   masticating
The slow clouds in their cuds

   Filling their boulder-thick bodies
With fog to make them light   the massive all-meat
   Haunches gliding on hooves of gold
The sensitive tendons   thin

   Ankles   those magical shock absorbers
Transferring weight to earth   one hoof raised perhaps
   Poised like the wrist of a ballerina
Or gently tapping for grass-

   Clumps   *A child's breath of dreams*
Envelops the peace of a mare   draws her into a human

Field   light-years of safety-alertness
Are lifted   a morning thought

Swerves... The child's lips
Are pressed to the skin of the house   blood runs
    In the plumbing the walls cave in cave
Out on the lungs of the bed his breath

    Unsettles the roof   a breathing
Without meets a breathing within   a mare and her colt
    Pasture in the yard   grass in their throats
Is hair of the child's head

    They lick his skin of the stones
The swing-ropes   their manes flow over tall weeds
    Of his limbs their delicate hooves
Tap at the soil of his cheek-

    Bones   kiss the gravel
Of his cranium   beg to be let in to be let in   and oh
    It is a floating   the horses and child
Aloft in the one house skin

Santana

The usual hazards seem to be worse this fall:
the Santana gales
escalate, in moments, massive bales
of tumbleweed like giant eagles' nests, uptorn,
and stampeding over the mesa. Some few seem to crawl
in and out of the steep ravine ditch,
to rise again in blurred puffs like unshorn
sheep, and leap the cyclone fence
as into my yard they pitch.
I, at my patio door, engulfed in trance.

This morning, dust in the kitchen's a half-inch thick.
The Los Angeles fire-
storm rages wider and higher,
devouring scores of acres of timber per minute
and as many Hollywood homes in an hour—that quick!
I stand at the doorstep. A newspaper cyclone
(the delivery boy hardly thought to begin it)
commences. The children whip by on skates. They stretch
pieces of sheeting for sails.
My neighbor prays they'll postpone
the nuclear war till his fallout shelter is finished.

(Each temblor and sonic boom wrests him with panic.)
He fumes after the gray,
wide, antisepetic garbage truck, sway-
ing in the wind like a female hippopotamus
in heat, its trail, the aftermath of a manic-
depressive: corrugated cans and their contents strewn
all about. (In the hands of an ignoramus
or two at the heads of State rests
the instantaneous fate of three billion human
lives. The harmless shapes of my domestic chaos suggest

that horror.) I find myself bounding across the lawn
in pursuit of a runaway
tricycle. From between my legs, with a display
of chagrin, emerges its huffing owner who unbalances
the would-be rescuer, and barely escapes being sat on
in the ensuing collapse. Before I'm back on my feet,
seven cartons blow past. What are the chances
for survival? A shake of the dice.
I reach in all directions at once, but end in defeat.
Let the wind take all. My breath has turned to ice.

My Father Dreams of Baseball

On hot September nights, when sleep is scarce,
in place of sheep Dad counts home runs that carry
the left-field fence and fly clean out of the ball park.

    Father snaps off the twi-night doubleheader;
    Behind his back, the screen door loosens a hinge.
    He escapes to the backyard retreat to rant at the ump.
    Hopped-up in the Porsche, he's off for an all-night binge.
    By morning, Mother's throat has a telltale lump.
    He takes his losses hard, a heavy bettor.

In his dreams, white dashing figures circle the bases.
Their caps dazzle in the sun like lights on a scoreboard.
The diamond is worn a foot deep under hammering cleats.

    He attends home games. Through Dad's binoculars
    the power hitters charge home plate like bulls,
    and make the picador pitcher's heart stand still.
    (A curve ball is a lance that bull's-eyes skulls.)
    My father in the stands directs the kill
    like a black matador in Madrid spectaculars.

Just inches inside the foul line, a figure is poised
three feet in the air, his arm outstretched for the catch.
His mouth is pinched with the pain of a near-miss.
The features are fixed with the dull metallic glow
of an ancient face, cast in bronze or brass.

Black Lotus of the Links

On the patchwork fairways of Rackham
and Palmer Park, we follow the Blacks.
Mandy (short for Ozymandias)
swings a homemade driver with a half-
pound lead slug insert under the club
face. Zeke (for Ezekiel) lumbers
under thirty-seven unmatched clubs
scrambled in a sun-cracked, squat beer keg
strapped to his back with a pair of tattered

suspenders. The foursome assembles
at the first marker. Zoro (after
Zoroaster) addresses his ball,
propped on a six-inch sterling silver
tee. Hunched like a cornered elk, his stance
flat-footed, he lurches forward. His
silhouette is a boxer throwing
a fast uppercut. The image blurs.
A cap pistol report echoes. The ball

vanishes with a hiss. Luke, the last
of the quartet, smells of Scotch. He hugs
his bag with ardor, cradles it down,
touches a ball to his lips for luck,
and bends from the waist, a hip flask
bulging his pants, to tee the ball up.
His eyes shut; the long arc of his swing
is an arm that circles his lover's
waist. The perfect meeting of ball and club-

head is noiseless: "Sweet hit!"
                                    Their shadows,
epileptic, seem to continue
into their clothes, fill them, and run out

at their necks and sleeves. *Exhalations*
of a moist earth, half-asleep in their
skins, they dance across fairways like black
rivers of the dawn.
Prone to the green,
Zeke lines up his putt. He is wrinkled
tarpaper. Upright for the stroke, stalwart,

he is velvet Midnight. His eyes are moons.

Corners

The whole man has no corners. He curves and curves.
Whatever goes in comes out the other side, or stays in

And takes his shape. Wherever you start in himself
You come back to the same place. But it isn't the same. The skin

Of his eyes is safe to touch. If he cuts, he is not sharp.
Take the bird stuck in my office one day this summer.

I opened all the windows. He was furious.
He had to concentrate hard to fall through the closed

Windows. He was busy dissolving his atoms, one by one,
To squeeze through the glass. I must have confused his thinking.

Whenever I opened a window he flew to the next
Closed one, until there were no more to open.

Then he swung from wall to wall, from ceiling to floor,
Bruising his wings in the corners, and shrieking.

I leaned on the wall for support, to hear myself trying to cry.
If I fell from my mind for a moment, the floor would press me

Into the wall, my belt or my tie stuck in the corner,
Tugging me square in my body, or square on one side.

It would take just a minute. I ran from the room. I came back
To check on the bird. He was gone. Now this is true.

When I left, the corners softened to curves, and the room grew round.
The bird slid back into the world in a soft arc of lamentation.

Skin Song

I cannot be a fish   sure of failure, I will try
no risk, no loss

the flippers tell my feet   flesh, be rubber
you must not bend or kick   to be
moved, lie still   to be held
let go

the mask instructs my face
mouth, stay shut   the Other
opens   be slow, nose
you will breathe
easy   eyes
do not be first, come
after   late, you will see more

Water commands:

body, be light   the will
is heaviness   ignorance
has no weight   know
nothing   give everything away   cast off
self to the deep   shed weight
lightness   grows
full   body, be light

be white, blood   be
without color   lose your red
grow lighter than water
thinner   blood, be white

skin, be empty   sleep
you will dream

a motion not your own   a motion
that is given   give
up, touch   be taken   emptiness
lifts   skin, be empty

Transvestite

I must undo my robes of the air,
    untie my earth-
  cloak
of foreignness, step out of my fear-being,
    ease into my sea
  skin
of a fish. I must enter my salt-self,
    drawing the smooth
  current
about me like heavenly drapes.
    A brainy stranger,
  I divest
crew cut and gold fillings, the silver
    ring on my wedding
  finger
the water-tight wise ticker at my wrist
    proudly droning
  its one
secret to the wet world's deafness:
    Time's muffled
  bees' buzzing.
I must unremember my name, my birthplace,
    the number on my license
  plates,
my address, the brand of my children's
    toothpaste, the blessed
  earth-smell
of my wife's hair: to belong here,
    I become a nameless
  dumb
free and easy man-thing. A presence
    infinitely deep
  blue-green,
full, rain-caressive, invites me,

opens to one just
opening
up, who, not now as a lame
    stranger, may
enter.
I take in my hands all, all
    that I touch,
    and leave
no fingerprints. No signature.

Tarpon

Five shadows in heavy motion, lumbering half-seen,
  pass me on either side, shark
panic slowly leaving my fluttered breath pumping as I make

  out the tarpons' armored plate scales,
diamonded in silvery weave, the undershot bulldog
  jaw, his thick cylindrical body,

a wingless fuselage, famed for muscling twelve foot
  leaps in the air on his tail's pole
vault—when hooked, and broadjumping thirty feet at a bolt,

  many times, in Kodak-flash succession.
Now some thirty tarpon pass, in clusters of three to six.
  Still mindful of shark fins, I half-spin

radially, peering from side to side, with metronomic
  evenness of rhythm, kicking to and fro
to sustain a stable axis of pivot, the only way to keep

  from drifting blindly out of shore's safe
keeping, my attention fastened undivertedly to the man-sized
  passersby. I scrutinize the larger specimens,

ruling out the offchance of a lone predator, prowling.
  I take heart finally, as the school thins
out, a few last (three foot!) small fry trailing behind,

  solitarily, one pausing just under my legs,
looking after the others, and up at me disconcertedly,
  finally edging up to my spear for a closer

view . . . a being more innocent, quiet, curious—more frail
   than myself. My hand, before my very eyes,
puts down claws: all the violence I so dreaded to find,

   moments before, in a fancied pursuer, now
surging in my arm, up my back and neck, and finally,
   shaking my eyes in my skull like false

teeth in a cup. I hang back. The loaded speargun,
   its three rubbers taut for release,
jiggles between us, seemingly playful, fish-chumming

   away the tarpon's caution, a kinship
springing up between us; my hand still shaking its fury,
   becomes a strange brute thing, self-motivated,

disengaged, yet clinging still to my wrist, tugging
   at my joints as a mad dog on a leash,
yearning for a sickening engagement: *my eyes fix*

   on a point above his head, drilling in.
A brain shot would yank him up, so much limp flesh
   hung on a spit; a tail shot implode

all fierceness inside him, our two nerve cords thrown
   into a queer freedom of naked contact,
as though our bodies had fallen away, and the nerves

   danced and leapt and wound about each
other like quivering vines . . . I have been here before.
   I have dreamed the death of friends, died

in a friend's dream, and come back. For love, I could
    kill, or be killed. I'll always return,
as a fish perhaps, as myself turned fish. Fish-friend,

    I drop my spear. All terror, love, thee
I spare, who can tow a twenty-foot sailing smack
    for hours, or twist and snap a heavy

duty wrought-iron spear like a pretzel, or tug
    an ill-fated spearfisherman to breath-
less lung-forfeiting depths . . . In seconds flat.

The Coral Reef

The sea is a circuit of holes:
mouths, bellies, cavities in coral-heads,
caves, deep cracks and wedges in the rock.
Brain coral stipple the bay meadows like toadstools,
each a community in siege. Shellfish, so frail,
secrete rock-skeletons,
rainbow-jeweled. These build. Rain, wind, the waves,
and boring animals corrode the sculptured lime,
dissolving the reefs to sand-deposits. The parrot
fish puckers his lips for love, and gnaws
death-kisses into coral.

Snorkelers hug the surface.
Divers scout gingerly among the poisonous
antlers, knowing the lightest brush with fire-coral
draws blood and raises the flesh in welts: the pores
look out like portholes from the swellings. The sting
in each seems individual.
Coral-wounds are coated with slime, fish-slippery.
They are slow to heal . . . In murky waters, sun blinds.
Sun trapped in snows of plankton glares like headlights
on wet asphalt, the white on the gray, light blocking out
sight. The scuba-diver

collides with a wall of fry,
so thick with sliver-fish the luminous flanks
seem impervious, but his waving spear-end glances
not one fish on any side, the weightless flakes
dodging and veering, the larger movement of Overall
undeflected by internal
shifts. The school is running from gamefish: jack,
mackerel, gar, tarpon—they in turn pursued by predators:
shark, barracuda *no smile that curve of the jaws,*

an accidental twist of the gum-cartilage:
a chilling glance commands

　an instance that power needn't
be linked to size. grip speargun. if you shoot, don't miss
the head. spear in the tail. power mower gone berserk.
the handle cannot steer the blades. the head
a madly chopping bushel of teeth, wobbly.
weaving about the spear as axis.
as one who juggles a sixty-pound two-edged machete
under water. Trigger-finger shifts to the shutter.
Camera-shy fish and cuda-shy man, matched
for the moment, eye one another (neither advancing
to test the other's nerve),

　look away, look back. Cuda
turns! Barrel-length torpedos from sight!
Now, overhead, three Oldwife (Queen Triggerfish)
sail past, like kites. Wide and flat, they cannot
swim straight on, but turn spasmodically
from right to left, in squad
formation, cutting across their own paths,
and across his line of sight, narrowing to thumb's-
widths as they crisscross his axis, diplaying one profile,
now another (*flash. discard bulb.*): triangular snouts
and trapezoidal posteriors,

　the graceful semiparabolas
of dorsal and ventral fins, the axehead tail.
The man, tank on his back, descends. From seafloor
he peers under a shelf. In an inverted socket,
a lobster, the elusive female, her tail curled
on itself, conceals her treasure:
the orange bushel of eggs, blossom of caviar.

Her bubble-eyes on stalks (or stilts) look backward
behind her head, see around corners—they stare
and stare. The antennae, like a blindman's fingers
in the dark, must touch to tell.

   Dodging antennae, the diver
squirms into snapshot range. *large spiny forelegs.*
a male's. thrust over the lens. followed
by wide armored head. gloved hand traps leg—it drops
from body-joint. inert. like head of burnt match.
backwards lunge: muscular
tail contracts. scuffle of spear-jabs. pronged
back disengaged in a last rally of spasms.
drifts limp to the bottom. Halfway down,
the swarm are upon him, small nibblers lovingly
smooch and probe, their bites

   kiss-languid, entranced,
tenderly scooping flesh from shell, the carcass
suspended in skilled dismemberment, no part
touching bottom unemptied. Death-gyps! The dying
members, portioned into living guts, *survive,*
survive. Suddenly, the ledge
under his flippers sways, no footrest. Step off.
Move gently. The rock's alive, thousands of coraleyes,
feelers *busy busy,* tireless reef-toilers. Note
sponge, anemone, barnacle—lovely in their private
sleeps—malingerers these,

   parasites of the colony, taking
a free ride; the workers *the small,* drawing out of dun
selves mounds of iridescence: minuscule bodies
hatching, in fury of survival, gorgeous refuse, careless
towers of jewels, wreaths of rock-tissue, mouth's

masonry, flowers of fire . . .
At dawn, peering from a light-weight Cessna, cruising
low over the clear bay shallows, the water brutally
calm, the horseshoe-shaped reef entirely in view,
the beholder deciphers the expressions of an aging face,
chiseled by love. Dumbfounded,

he is pierced with reverence.
The Saint-edge margin, Life/Death, fades, dissolves
in his eyes, *dreams: a boy's fishhook waiting,*
waiting to make wounds, to tug, to snap off in the big one
lost, to go deep, to die into life, to lie there in rich
corrosion, iron becoming
a part of the fish, the small hard thread of metal
breaking down and entering every canal and cell,
lastly into teeth, fins and scales. Intestines
are intelligence: such skill in distribution—equally—
to every pocket of life.

FROM

The Osprey
Suicides

1973

The Diving Ballet

For Binnie

No one
Can teach us the deep-water
Moves—we are swimming a dance to music
We cannot hear in our heads.
We hear

With our skins.
Holding hands to keep from drifting
Apart, we try to embrace. We brush lips.
But a nearer thing than each
Other,

A kissing
Of many skins, is wrenching
Us out of our two-ness. In water suspended,
Our bodies are inside and out
Of themselves.

As I fall,
You rise. It is a diving
Ballet. Above, you break surface. Below,
Leaning to stay down,
I touch

Bottom—
Thinking, can this be earth?
I am flying so close to a floor whose one
Will is to send me back, feet
First, to a ceiling

Of wind.
I resist, dreaming myself

Empty; weightlessness holds like an anchor.
Now overhead, motionless,
You shadow me,

Belly-floater!
Instantly, you lunge, tumbling—
Taken by impulse, you are set free in your body,
Head flung back, back-
Somersaulting

In a long arc,
A slow-rolling lyric sweep.
As I rise below you, I see in your upside-
Down face curving up to me,
Circling

Up from under you,
The adventure your body, newly
Strange, is beginning to believe in, in
Love with itself. For minutes,
You do not breathe.

You see in,
Looking out. Something within you
Is swimming beyond, getting further ahead
The more slowly it strokes.
Your mind

Must slow down
To catch up. In spaces between
No-breaths, you are learning to hear the waves
Of your pulse cross the Self-
Abyss.

Lobsters in the Brain Coral

Freediving thirty to forty feet, only a few seconds to spare
at the bottom of each dive before the death
    of my wind, I catch sight of an antenna or front leg-pincer
waving listlessly into the light like a weed-stalk:

    the only visible appendage of a tough old bull langouste,
his spiny-thorned carapace of back wedged deep
    into a crevice in steep flat near-vertical planes of rock.
His trench lightless, I can only guess his position—

    impossible to snare him with a gig-noose, I aim the Hawai-
ian sling spear, stretched taut on the bow of my forearm.
    The spear connects, freezes. I hustle to the surface for air,
hyperventilate, and dive again; hanging upside-down,

    my legs dangling over my head, I peer deeply into the cleft.
No sign of life. Hah!—he's braced for the fight.
    Tugging and tugging at the spear, I yank out his twenty-
pound impaled barrel-shell, his crotchety long legs

    wriggling—he looks like a Gargantuan subaqueous spider!
He contracts his muscular powerful tail,
    discharging high-pitched cries that seem to emit
from a sphere of sound surrounding him, a queer

    distancing remove between the creature and its shrieks.
I compress the tail. He silences. The spear
    runs deep into his back, diagonally. I force the point,
flared-open within him, through to the other side

    and unscrew the spearhead, his great armored body-vault
shuddering quietly. Astonished by his suffering,
    his austere beauty, I relax my grip—he jerks loose,
scraping his backspikes across my bare wrist,

three streaks inscribing my skin. *The red ink smears,*
runs, thinning off into swirls, a spreading
      stain. Slow leaks—painless—from my punctured inner tubes,
I deflate. Oh stop, precious flow. A blow-out,

      I may go flat, caving-in on my bones. The lobster zooms
backwards, his tail flapping—violent, noiseless—
      his body a single bony claw swiftly clenching, unclenching,
his whines a siren wailing softer in the distance.

      In pursuit, I chase him below a massive brain coral. I swim
under a grayish bulge and drift into the interior,
      my hand gripping the rim. Am I staring inside somebody's
dream? In five or six rooms of his skull—

      sockets like sinuses, honeycombing the coralhead—stand
lobsters of all sizes: some upside-down,
      others on the walls, the floor; always in the dark
corners, favoring the shadows, leaning away

      from the light, antennae waving. I move my glove
to the nearest cubicle, and tap a pincer.
      It falls from the body. The lobster drops out of sight
into a hidden channel. Then, the whole colony

      move in unison: bodies uplifted, legs stretched taut,
unbending, all begin sidling in a slow trot
      around the linings of the caverns, a dance of skinless
bones, creakless many-jointed rickety stilts

      dragging the glossy-plated bodies this way and that,
somersaulting over and over, sagging
      without letting go, until I forget if my feet are under
or over my head. Let me out of your brain,

I command the dreamer. I suffocate in this airless hive
where I lose my mass in your sleep. Awake!
My weight drifts, fades to a gas in your mind.
Do I decompose? *You become an enamelled box*

on spindly crutches. Lay out your fingerprints lengthwise
and braid them into two feelers—antennae.
Fly backwards, snapping your whip of tail; your tail
the one muscle, the one hatchery, the one edible.

Wail, if attacked. When cornered, back to a wall,
drop off your legs, twiggy stick by stick,
flop in the gravelly bottom-muck, a glum squat egg,
quadruple amputee. A basket case. Give me back

to my jails of skin, to my soaps of blood-suds, to my glands,
lungs and lymphs, to all those emerald birds—
heart, liver, gall bladder and balls. Oh spheres and cubes
of my body, multiply strangely into diamonds

whose many shining stars are eyes, eyes that glow,
eyes that radiate light but admit no spark—
eyes luminous, eyes opaque—a universe of eyes sparkling
in another's dream. Eyes of my flesh, restored!

Flying Below Sea Level

After hours under water, a mask
    for face,
        air is a ceiling,
and sky a comfortable myth,
    like heaven.
        Sun, a film
of white-hot molten light,
    floats
        on the surface,
like oil. It will scald my scalp
    if I rise—
        to get my breath.
Here and there, planes of light
    intersect
        the surface, knife
the upper field, and fan out
    in shelves.
        In shallows, they strike
bottom, spilling rainbow
    all about
        the coral. There
are brains in the fish's tail
    (alert
        for messages), the fins
are nerves, each scale a fingertip . . .
    My cheek,
        slapped by a moulded
soft-spongy mass, half-moon
    shaped—
        gently stinging—
I dodge a gelatin-trio, running
    with the current
        faster than I can
swim away. Then, I'm surrounded

by hordes,
        mounds bumping
each other, sliding around me—
        painless
            between my legs,
across my face. Wherever I
        look, the sea
            is milky-translucent,
separate outlines no longer
        visible.
            The water, gelling
into a vast slug-slimy pudding—
        impenetrable—
            half-carries me along
(a man-blob swallowed in viscid
        ooze), half-
            disgorging me,
by turns. I dive, down-thrust
        through a hole
            opening just under
me, swim below the flying island
        of jelly,
            and enter the under-
water cave. I hear a high-pitched
        crackling,
            like dry twigs
burning, on all sides enclosed
        by a soundless
            hush. I hang,
motionless, at the center of the cave:
        magnetized . . .
            I am seen
by thousands of unseen eyes!
        I shudder

at a burst of color:
a large hogfish, bright scarlet-
orange, appears;
high-finned, majestic,
wide and flat, brilliant-sheened;
seeming twice
its size, swelled
in enclosure. No change in his wide-eyed
elongated
hog-snout at sight
of me, no change in his glide-rhythm,
he picks up
speed as he spins,
circling the interior of the cavern;
so nervous
to escape me, he misses
the exits, tunnels, again and again.
The space
around me expands.
Light from no source filters up
from depths
without bottom.
I grow larger and larger. The cave
I filled
fills me. As I wind,
snake-easeful, back through the cave-
mouth, I
feel the whole sea
tilt to fill the missing space.

Skin-Flying into the Storm Center

Wary of lightning,
we dodge the thundercloud's blue-black
center—the sky overhead pulsating feeble glimmers—
swimming across the current to escape
the heavy drift tugging us back
into the gray storm-patch.
We are alert for the whirring
steel propeller knives of the
French
fishing skiffs, their skippers
dozing; to the ear of a submerged diver,
the whine of the outboard
motors is a power mower in the distance,
up close an electric handsaw: we hug the surface!
A quartermile downcurrent, a tall vertical
flickering shadow appears—
too low for a cloud.
We make out meteoric flashes
of white against sky's pearlgray,
blurred swirls of activity.
We are pulled nearer. Zigzagging traceries
become arcs of tails
and wings twirling like leaves
in a wind-whipped elm: a flock of gulls and frigate birds,
packed so thick they block out light
like a storm-cloud, chasing
vast schools of fish.
We swim closer, closer.
Needle-beaked streaking darts!
The frigate birds, streamlining
their forked scissorstails, nosedive for fish.
Now bird-beaks whiz
past my ear, just under my mask-
glassed nose. A sword-blade plunges before my eyes,

trailing a beady-eyed undersized ball peen
head, tail feathers vanishing;
the reversed sword emerges
tipped over, gliding hori-
zontally: it skims the surface,
dragging a wildly convulsive
high-backed king mackerel, twice the length
and weight of its captor.
Remarkably, the beak dismembers
the backflesh and swallows without loosening its iron-
clamp grip.
From all sides, a dozen-odd gulls attack,
stripping clean the exposed fish-
skeleton, while the helpless
carrier-bird makes futile
sideways dashes to escape,
unable
to salvage any gob of its prey.
Many gulls thwack into the carcass with furor,
the lifeless fish quaking
more violently than when it gave up
its last life-spasms to the single killer beak—still hold-
ing
firm, despite the simultaneous concussion
of numerous rivals striking
the same last traces
of meat-flakes from bones.
Voracious, they seem to aim
for each other's necks and skulls,
but zeroing in from all angles—even below—
each hits the mark.
A sharkfin cuts through the slaughter-
bloodied rainbow sea. Flipper-flapping madly, we lunge
from the murky bloodlake into crosscur-

rents.
      Swiftly, we are taken by four knots
   of current—holding our arms
and legs like rudders, we learn
     to keep steady, steering a few
       degrees
  against the mainstream
  like sailboats tacking into the wind. Now we pass
directly into the eye
of the storm. We sense the current
  reversing—a few strokes further—without surface signals.
     Just ahead and below, I see fish lean
      sharply
        at an angle, or am *I* turning
    sideways? Now the fish
  lie flat on their sides,
      struggling back up, to turn
       upright,
   but falling away . . . Suddenly,
  we are stunned by stillness—a deep hush in the air.
We are motionless.
The absence of current is chilling . . .
Skin sleeps. Air is a vacuum to us. When the wind
    blows, do we think, air-thick: *it is this*
      we take in and puff out each moment
    of life? With this
  we ignite the calories,
     burning them to bones and brains!
   Listen. *Her appetites*
 will never be satisfied. She is wife of the storm
and mother to capricious
gusts. Too thin to melt,
  too fine to cut a petal, this chaste pool's elusive.
    Her issue can choke a whale, hew mountains,

reverse the pattern of seas
and continents.
She files her teeth on shale.
    But the skin sleeps, won't touch
her fierce invisible waves . . .
Slosh, slosh—all at once the rain floods
down on our heads.
In fear of drowning, absurdly,
  we drop masked faces in the sea. Just under the surface,
    preternatural blue-gray stillness! Above:
     fingers of ice run over
   our necks and backs.
  Pure salt-free taste. A solid
    rainwall gushing froth, a surf-
     floor
  everywhere continuous:
  cold, density, rage and blindness . . .
Below: warmth,
airy thinness, ghostly calm.
  Crystallinity to all depths: every particle glint-edged,
    striated with color; all angles and curves
     of minutiae insistent to the eye,
    disseveral. Allseeingness!
  Incandescence! The self—
    a luminous subterranean eye—
  spreading like sight, radiating
hundreds of feet in all directions from the storm
   center.

The Spearing

Who am I chasing—underwater—in my life?
When I spear a fish in the face,
Do my own eyes
Stare back
As the life rushes out?
My best friend's eyes? Or my wife's?
Is the wish to see pain I make in the face

Of a loved one akin to murder? Does the blood
In my erection leave blood on my hands?
Are you in love with
My death
Of you? When we cook
The fish, do you eat the eyes?
They will stab you, just under the heart.

Why do you *eat* so much? Swollen and massive,
A great Jewfish, do you turn
Your back to me
All night
And wait to be skewered,
Looking behind with fantastic
Puffy face? When I dived for the lovely

Pompano—with majestic jutting head—
You looked after me 'til I spun
Out of sight, spiralling
Down—Oh
I went too deep,
And something burst in my head
Like a grenade as I kicked to the surface,

But my eardrums walled out the blast. At night,
You tickled your love in my ears,

Talking and purring
It would be
All right. By morning,
I was stone-deaf, your tongue
All spotted with blood, a lover's knife.

Increasing Night

His empty heart is full at length,
But he has need of all that strength
Because of the increasing Night
That opens her mystery and fright.
                    —W. B. Yeats

I get closer to the dream, trying to remember
What happened and to learn which of the accidents outside
Became parts of my urgent inner life,
When my attention lags and the wrong lines

From a beloved somebody else's trouble invades my page—
Whose heart's occlusions usurp my heart's—
And all my tongue's wrestlings and wranglings to translate
The flames of my dream's furnace

Into mirroring music are hopelessly garbled.
The great effort with which I rage to forget Love
And Lord are my stubbornest lies to outsmart is stupidly
Heroic, for all my crimes of loving

And sins of prayer are a pale cover-up
For the ear's guilt of deafness to the dream's call,
For the mouth's guilt in turning away
From sleep's lips kissing the brain awake,

For the hand's guilt in absentmindedly (but never accidentally,
There are no accidents!) relaxing its grip,
Breaking the vision's handshake, dropping the mountaineering
Twin brother-in-the-spirit

Headlong on his daily plunge to the death
From the precipice of waking
Into the bottomless gulch of irrecoverable ghostlife,
The secret life I am overkind to friends

Falsely every day to forget I am failing, the failed
Dream all my success unsuccessfully hides
Or numbs until sleep
The incorruptible arsonist (just try to bribe

Or buy *him* off, just try!) sets fire
To no matter how many faces I've donned and doffed
In losing battles with the permanent mask spreading
Like cancer-blooms under my selfafraid eyes.

Inside the Gyroscope

For Deborah

Daughter, this is our laughing-box:
a gyroscope orbiting us
two ways at once—
top to bottom, left to right. I try to relax
and enjoy the scares, to roll
with the machine's laughing gears—the computerized gentle
terrors, but shock kills my cackles:

I freeze like a funnybone
when the bumped elbow's burning nerve tickles
the length of your arm, and the skin—
pricked with a thousand
pins—tingles. As we sail
through the wider arc of the tilting Great Wheel,
our eggshell cage, an ellipsoid

spinning on its axis, hurtles me
upon you; my weight—
stone in a sling—pinning you sideways against our satellite's
grillewire, your legs tangled under,
frail wings flapping: "Daddy,
you take the steering bar,
give us a rough ride, make us twist

and twist." Now we halt,
trapped in the middle of a reverse somersault,
careening, heels over heads,
rocking on the base of our skulls. We are staring straight
up, fifty feet to the ground,
into three ovoids—family faces—high overhead
and directly below us:

mother and sister O-mouth gapes, the wailing face
of your brother, whose helium
balloon has fallen
up, up, up (I nearly capture the string,
its lifeline, poking
two fingers through the wiremesh
grate) and drops skyward

under our legs, shrinking
to an agate, a green pea, a pinhead
trailing a hair; it sails into a cloud, vanishing . . .
I waken from a wacky dream. Stepping from bed
in the dark, I slip on the soft
bumps of my daughter's hips and head.
Must I walk on walls to spare her pain? When I lift

her to carry her back
to bed, the chill of the floor
passes from belly to belly. She is winning her war
with sleep—a rage to stay awake!
A little past midnight, she embarks on nocturnal tours:
I hear a soft pitter-patter like a mouse
under floorboards. She cartwheels

from room to room—practices
handsprings, headstands for Saturday tumbling class.
Like a wind-up toy, its spring coiled to the snapping point,
she never unwinds.
She rummages about the great toy-bin
of our house, moony-eyed, alchemizing our leaden nights
into goldened lonely second

days. She never lies down.
Sleep must overtake her in mid-play, standing up.

I find her in odd corners at sunup:
on the second shelf of the linen closet, half-awake,
buried in washcloths, towels; under the sofa,
the face of the lion rug curled over her ear, its sunflower
yellow whiskers licking her cheek.

Love, the Barber

Love, the barber, shaves the night fields.
He trims the forests. Between his blades

Fall waves of the sea. They calm themselves.
Whatever falls away grows back in another

Place, in sleep. Beautiful hanks. My wife
Cuts my daughter's hair. Oh, it hurts my eyes

At first. Sweet face, you look so bare.
The brute has severed locks of sleep, and weightless

Dreams are falling fast, oh fast; the floor
Is strewn with waves of softest curls.

Let us walk there, only if we must. Step
Lightly. What fell from you I lift

In my hands—through stumbling
Fingers slip your thinnest strands.

2

Love, the barber, eats down to the roots. Clip, clip.
Yes. I swear the air has teeth some nights

And chews the fields, but not from hunger.
Some bites caress the wound, and heal like death . . .

My students are cropping their long hair shorter,
Not short, lifting just over their once-covered

Shoulders, their necks still hidden. No ears.
Thought, unspoken, waves through the classroom,

Curls, and in curling, straightens our backs.
My idea, a tight braid, unties, shakes loose.

We are revising our poems. I can be happy to collapse
Into my lines, the furrowing lines in my forehead.

We lift crooked faces. All together—this moment—
We are growing back our lost features.

Homage to Austin Warren

1. *At the Book Sale: A Memory*

A leatherette relic smelling of musk and camphor falls

Open in my cup of hands to a zany overmarked
Page: there is
No mistaking the scrawled marginalia of Austin Warren
Crowding the print off the page,

Demanding, insisting, bickering in a kingly true lover's
Tiff over word flesh-and-blood, I am swept
Back into the aura of that raspy
Voice   slow-gurgling   weighted down by tonnage
Of learned reference
Warren's voice—unmistakably no one else's—blazing into memory

As I pore over the remarks in a worried
Black script, penned in that familiar, crabbed, near
Illegible hand (whether difficult

From nerves, illumination, or sheer weight of mind

On edge I was never to know)   I recall
I'd chewed for hours like a dog on a pant leg
At obscure marks on themes, some words
Beginning with odd caps placed wrongly   for emphasis
Which one my grade?   Somewhere   I

Guessed   in that barbwire alphabet   the clue to my future

2. *In Frontroom Chapel*

The summer I first winged words   sent them flying   arrows
Effortlessly zinging   feathered into being . . .

In the apartment upstairs,   I could not seem to open
My eyes wide enough to take
In the foreignness of frontroom chapel   breath-

Drugging incense smoke-curling up from the altar
The crucifixion   between wooden frames
Wire-hung on a bent hook   imperceptibly awry   the wine-
Maroon walls   papered unbrokenly   tier
Upon tier   with oilskin of bookbacks   outspreading
From floor to ceiling

                                who was it   who I
Kneeling at his feet   not in prayer   shakily   who
He   leafing pages of type-
Script   his high forehead scrunching at wrongnesses
Everywhere met   all efforts
To conceal the badness of words his eyes scanned
Failed
Who we   his one voice speaking
For two the sound coming or seeming to come from one point
Above and from another inside my head

Falling out of the room upper air
As out of a cloud

Our bodies   our lives in the present are strange
To us   of all the beings to whose lips he lifted my hands
His selves were the least known   a breath

From Shakespeare's nostrils warmed
My fingertips   there was room for Donne and me to share
Intimacies in Warren's one
Skin of his poems   sentences of Henry James

He spoke inflated the unused ear of my mind like a third lung air
Found in my second wind of hearing a better place

To stream   I took one step   from hearing to breathing one
Step   the trained ear flowering into voice
Shaking loose   my own voice   a blossom   opening

Song of the Thrush

In terror of my typewriter's greed for profit,
Tethered to business letters
Bleeding out of my hand, I hasten, a guest
Trespasser my beckoning neighbor

Halts, half out of my clothes half in, my face coloring
Before I can think *shame,* how much of me is showing

I cannot check now, but I feel cool
In two or three wrong skin
Places. Decoyed, I quit the public walk,
Prancing to the lawn, obedient

To her pointing finger, her lips including me in a message
I cannot hear over traffic, her husband beside her

Sighting directly on a branch at eye-level
Tail feathers: the first thrush
Of spring. Oh happy transport! I'm severed
By a cadence from the ambition magnet

Pulling my letters to the corner mailbox. Her face
Wound in its mystery, her arms folded for warmth

In the morning chill shift to a cradling
Motion as she explains how
Important the thrush music was each morning
Last spring when the nursing baby

Woke her at four. The thrush rescued her from petty
Anger, lifted her spirit, and deadened the worst

Acids of postpartum orneriness, her fifth
Offspring a boy at last,

Their last try taking more nerve than hope
After twin girls. Both past thirty-five.

Both saved. It is a joy to them for me to share their plunder
Of the bird they love. I bow to charities of the thrush.

Island Trashfires

Christmas: three tourist
liners in port, two more at anchor
in harbor
mouth; the largest,
a city-block long, eight ship-floors

high, triple-smokestacked. This year, jets
rival the old army transports,
three tail engines
rocketing into steep inclines
on takeoff. Hourly,

the Pan Am whisperjets plow furrows in runway
asphalt, motors reversing an air wall,
wingspan extending far over the parallel
service road, fuselage groaning to a stop
on the miniature landing strip.

The airstrip clings to the west
shore, a Band-Aid on a bruised wrist.
Adjacent to the garbage dump (an open sore
that drains the Island's poisons around the clock), old convairs
lift and lower

over trashfires
and the bellies of pedigreed
sharks—pampered, overfed, domesticated.
Inland, chicken-scrawny mongrels
pick about in the rubble for waste morsels.

In a sleep-daze of search,
they meander suicidally into onrush
of traffic . . . One airless hot night,

I drive to the airport road's unpaved dead end,
a skipping-stone's hurl

to the triple juncture
of water, runway and fainting bonfire.
Our hideaway fumes carrion-stink.
My carnivore hand swings
to fetch you, huddled

against your door.
In the lowered
headlamps, a three-legged terrier,
favoring its bandaged
stump, spots a tidbit just over the edge,

bobbing in shallows. The mutt
aims a short hop. We see a mako's lifted snout
jerk shut—the twitching furball, headless
in air, falls to the surface . . .
Vagrant drayhorses

and mules—no crops to plow,
no carts to haul—
are sold for children's sport, or abandoned
in backwoods. They drift over untilled farmland,
straying into paths of semis,

diesels . . . One morning, a half-starved donkey,
emaciated, is found roped to a tree, three arrows piercing
his belly; still alive on his feet, suffering
noiselessly; in his eyes,
absence, a luminous void. At the hairpin

curve, on the main drag to Island Top Mountain,
the overturned cement truck
lies smoking. Alongside the buckled hood,
a gray-and-white flecked
roan mare, legs splayed like old pipe cleaners under her bloated

abdomen, soaks in a pool of motor oil and blood.
A block or two below, a man about seventy,
with great, burl-knuckled hands, motions passing cars
to stop. The drivers, fierce-eyed, look away
from the poor whitetrash master

mechanic; southern expatriate from Tulsa
in faded cloud-pale blue
coveralls, he carries the secret of pure failure
("Failed brakes!") from car to car, curled in immaculate
vast hands like a jewel . . . Easter:

dawn traffic, slowed to a crawl—
no chance to pass on the serpentining downgrade—
bottlenecks. Midway on Rappune Hill,
the she-goats, their twitching hindquarters upraised
into motorists' faces,

thrust their narrow jaws
through gaps in fence wire. With languorous
tobacco-chawing sideways chops and grinds, they munch
the roadside clover, and won't be budged.
A ninety-year-old Anguillan,

the goat-boy, wags his pole at the stalled nannies.
As if dancing the tango
or conducting a minuet,
his arms, caressive and slow,
undulate.

The Osprey Suicides

Occasionally, an osprey locks its talons into a fish too large to handle and is pulled under to drown.

—Roger Tory Peterson

Casting from the Miami causeway
near Key Biscayne,
not a nibble
for hours into the sultry dawn (nor a scant gust,
no faint wind-whiffles),
my last tackle lost to heavy current and the bottom-
snags, I
empty the bucket
of live bait—squirming ten-legged shrimp—
lean over the concrete guardrail, and stare
into the water below. A blurred
shadow, flashing, rises from the depths;
distorted by its violent whirring,
the image seems oddly close to, as if
somehow above, the surface—
a ghostfish.
Now it hovers in one spot, halts, appears to settle
on the surface, stationary
but for a checkered dazzle of black-and-white splotches
blending
with the pale gray-white
reflection of the bridge—all image!

All's a mirroring, I think, as a soft
rhythmic swishing overhead
twists my neck in an abrupt upward reflex.
I'm arrested—checked and held—
by a brilliant osprey (the exact
twin of the mirrored
water-blur)
suspended on laboring wings, transfixed, as if impaled

on a fifty-foot pole.
Then he plunges headlong, leaving me staring into vacancy.
    My eyes,
      two arrows streaking
   for the target, race his plumb-line descent.
         He strikes the water—talons thrown forward
      on long white legs extended
        like pitchforks—the only visible prey
    is his own unblurred mirror-double:

the two birds, bilaterally symmetrical,
    collide, melting into
      each other:
both ospreys explode in foam! The powerful wingbeats
    breaking his dive
churn the surface into a wall of spray that hides all
      but outermost
    wingtips and beak
  held aloft, head never submerged.
        The wings, never folded, madly quicken,
     working ferociously for lift-off,
       as the bird slowly emerges from the cloak
    of foam—airborne at last—
clutching a large red snapper
   in his curled talons,
    his burden
losing drag, approaching weightlessness, while he gains
     speed and altitude.
       As he straightens
    into a vertical ascent,
  his water-image dims and shrinks,

      while a matching sky-image above, hanging
    immobile like a lantern projection

on the cloudscape, awaits his swift approach.
Grown distrustful of optic
fakes, I blink my eyes in wonder . . .
I look again.
As the climbing osprey diminishes in size, his perfected
sky-twin, unshrinking,
glides in a slow circle on extended wings. Before the lower
bird meets
his soul-brother in heaven,
the upper bird swoops down from above,
declaring himself a piratical bald eagle.
Trying to catch the osprey unawares,

the eagle homes in on him
and executes
a precision-timed swipe at the snapper. The smaller bird,
screaming his outrage,
swerves at the last possible instant, easily dodging clear
without halting—
or even appreciably
slowing—his rate of ascension.
The emperor of birds,
infuriated, soars quickly above the osprey,
again and again, whose masterful
side-veerings always deftly elude
the eagle dive-bomber's
aerial thrusts
as both raptors, hurtling like runaway kites into the upper
air,
are finally reduced
to little more than speckled motes against the sky. The osprey,
straining
to lift his freightage, climbs
slower and slower; his outleaps

grow fiercer; but at last
he drops the fish. The eagle, plummeting,
intercepts the falling carcass
just before it reaches the sea;
he glides
a few feet above sea level, flaunting his prize. Morning
trade winds arising,
I spot the osprey scanning the gusty bay
for surface game.
Following his search,
I notice a spread-winged highflier—
misidentified earlier
as obscure cloud-mirage—
now rapidly descending; he coasts

on motionless, vast, dark wings
outspread. Squinting
at the frigatebird's
unmistakable forked tail and webbed feet, I hardly notice
his side-slipping maneuvers
into position over the bald eagle. One savage pounce—
a bone-breaking
peck!—and his long
hooked beak instantly hijacks
the limp fish from the eagle's surprised claws,
old baldy bested by the man-of-war bird,
master of sky-to-sea pirates. The frigate
never alights on the water:
despite his onetime
water-strutting
webbed feet—now shrunken and held close to his body
on legs shortened
for total streamlining—he is unable to rise
from the sea

once fallen. The eagle
haltingly cruises downwind,

a dazed prince of the air drifting earthward.
The osprey keeps wending upward and outward, his
wings
a weft in the wind's shuttle,
his body lofted in broader circles
of a slowly upwinding
spiral.
He traces the periphery of an inverted cone with apex
near the bay's center,
extending his range of surface-tracking radar;
gauging
all points below
at once, he surveys a commanding
view of a great plain of water stretching
from shore to shore. Checking
himself at about one-hundred feet, he hovers—
a bombardier sighting his target—

and drops like a discharged projectile.
The shower of spray,
bubbling
higher and higher over the flapping wings, froths
like a small geyser
as the bird struggles to hoist
the payload
tugging him under.
The towering spume lowers, deflates,
when a blast of wind sucks his exposed wing
ends
and hurls him high over the swells
hefting a yards-long thick garfish,

                violently
whipping about, bending its wiry silverflanks double upon
        the talons piercing
    its back. As the osprey levels off,
        he coasts on a line
    parallel to the surface, perhaps five

                wingspans high. The strong head wind shifts
            course and fades; the osprey
                pivots to catch the last of the wind; wind
            dying, he surges nose-upward
    on strenuously heaving wingflaps,
        his claws buried
        in the gar's
spine, and sinking deeper, the fish jerking its tail in its
        last
        shimmering death throes.
I drop my eyes to the pair mirrored below, the reflected
        battle-
        thrashing of bird and prey
    strangely altered by optical alchemy
                into the amorous writhings of mating lovers,
            the upper figure alternately lifting,
                and being pulled down by the lower; but following
            a peak of vigorous flailing

    all motion quavers to a stillness.
        Before I can lift
        my eyes back
to the aerial pair, the aquatic pair has swallowed the original
        as echo drinks up sound.
    The osprey, collapsing on outstretched
            wings, falls
        into its image, still hugging
    its victim and slaughterer to its breast.

FROM

God's Measurements

1980

Kimono

Clonking up the cobbled roadway, I bob
And pitch on wood-slab clogs, my
Kimono sleazily mismatched under the twice-
Wrapped-round-my-middle sash. *Gaijin,* unkempt,
I halt, stopped by handmaiden's icy grace,
Who, with deft authority, ripping open
The dishevelled robes, unmasks my timid nudity.
A few swift tucks and shakes. The gown lies
Flat, seamless. Ah, maidservant, my bones
Go soft, collapsed and flattened, a hundred ribs
Smoothening under my soft silkskin.

Daibutsu

"Do not handle or climb on statue. Some people believe it is sacred
and venerable object. [Entrance to statue interior below, one
flight steps down stairs. Price ten yen.]"

—Kotokuin Temple, Kamakura

We are standing—
empedestaled—inside the God's
bronze head. Winding slowly up two
cramped narrow flights of stairs,
we have risen

spiralling into the great hollow
brain-vault, scaffolded into nirvana!
Tiptoeing onto the raised platform, our arms
outstretched, we place our feet with care—the steps
vertebrae of a two-story-high seated and cross-legged divinity's
spinal column. We run our fingertips along seams, marvelling
over wrist-thick welded sutures joining gray-olive-green
tarnished metal skull-plates. Ourselves surprised,
we are foreign bodies—transplants—

two queerly displaced
upright oblongs, giddy and pious.
Our tongues take root in the Buddha's
medulla oblongata; our timid
hushed voices,

magnified, bounce from wall to wall
of the vast cranial and thoracic echo-chambers:
God, statue & cathedral are of the one body, a hollow
clerestory in the church-nave of the colossus' shoulders.
Beginning our descent, we peer from the back through a single barred
window overlooking the sacred courtyard of the temple grounds—
burnt or beaten flat by fires and one great tidal wave

in this century leaving only the God intact,
though tinseled and ornamented

with sargassum, nori-
seaweed streamers, all manner of sea-
wrack, driftwood, roof-tiles, disheveled
bed-linens, kimonos, draperies . . .
Now we survey the wide

loft within the concave vaulted breast.
I am startled by the spectral figure of a doll-
sized deity, miniature squat replica of the whale-Buddha
through which we navigate our Jonah rites of passage, supported
on a small platform in a shallow recess of the rib-cage wall opposite.
It stares up at us: no mere fetus, but a scaled-down midget God,
offspring with identical features of the parent colossus;
the tiny mirror-image figure no infant divinity
but an ingested surrogate mind's-eye,

interior guardian
of the great Daibutsu! We
have entered the grand divine corpus
and meet Him face-to-face
within His own body

chambers. Mother, you have come,
knowing my untold need. Together, taken
into the God's cavernous integument and dumbfounded
by his spellbinding eye, at once, we hover in the single
good lung—though it, too, failingly—that kept my father alive
for our last best ten family years, and the resounding
boom of the gong we hear is a great sigh my father
heaves with his one good lung ballooning
around us, coming back in the God's

barrel-chested breath.
Oh, I know that wheeze and rasp
of phlegm & the surpassing joy of each
forced-breath taken in love of us,
so sweet his ease of heart

with each pained insuck of air,
and we know ourselves lifted in my father's
four-years-bereft stertorous wind-bag, the pleura
membrane of his good lung pulsating, fluttering in the God's
embronzed thorax; and here, in this heaving peace of an unearthly
metal-alloy aspiration, inhaling our recombined newly dead,
we three are born again in the stale crypt-foul Orient
air of a mammoth acoustics chamber, amphi-
theater of eternal return.

God's Measurements

(Todaiji Temple, Nara)

"The statue weighs 452 tons, measures 53.5 ft. in height, and has a face 16 ft.
long by 9.5 ft. wide, eyes 3.9 ft. wide, a nose 1.6 ft. high, a mouth 3.7 ft. wide,
ears 8.5 ft. long, hands 6.8 ft. long, and thumbs 4.8 ft. long. The materials
employed are estimated as follows: 437 tons of bronze; 165 lbs. of mercury; 288
lbs. of pure gold; 7 tons of vegetable wax; and an amazing amount of charcoal
and other materials."

— *Japan: The Official Guide*

As incense smoke thins, a stupendous,
     wide, brooding face emerges above us. The long ribbon-looped
ears, ending in weighty teardrop-
     fat lobes, slowly unravel from the wrappings of smoke trails
as we advance, the whole bronze olive-green head
     mushrooming from its mask
          of mist. It floats, hovers—balloonlike, isolate—
over the befogged shoulders. A cosmos
     of global body,
          seated cross-legged on a great lotus-
          blossom bronze pedestal, ascends

into the clearing before us,
     the pedestal in turn installed on a broader stone base
which knows touch of our hastily donned
     slippers, blocking our passage. Not one forward step possible,
we backstep twice to see the more clearly
     over the jutting head-
          high edge of stone, the full figure now vivid
and preternaturally clear before us,
     body draped in swirls
          of cloud, itself cloud-shaped, cloud-alloyed,
          growing into a mass, a solid—
if wavery—form. Still, it is the head,

so distant, holds us. Why do we so thrill at eye-guessed
estimates of measurements, measurements!
The eyes and mouth, wide as you are long, my son; the length
of ears makes two of you, the height of lofty face
three of me, and, yes,
you could ride lying on the thumb, your near mate
for length and width, the two of you nestled
together mimicking
a God's freakish double thumb! But, no, I
will not lift you to the stone ledge,

launching your unstoppable climb
to test my twin-thumbs caprice, despite your scandalous wails
reverberating in the temple
upper chambers, strident in my ears; nor shall I scold
or muzzle you, but hoist you to my shoulders
where, first clasping hands
for lift and support as you unfold to your full
height above my head, I clench your ankles,
as much to steady
and balance you as to prevent surprise
leaps. Together, of a tallness

to match, or exceed, the whole hand's length,
let us promenade around His Excellency's right flank.
Now, wobblingly, we stalk: you, stiltjack,
in love with instant towers sprung from the idiot body's
endlessly stretchable elastic of flesh, I
half scaffold, half anchor,
the two of us a father-son hobbling hinge—
telescope of our bones, joined end to end,
not doubled up
in laughter or loss of balance but bending
and unbending into beatitudes . . .

We look up, to scrutinize the God, stilt-
    walking our charmed gavotte. Then, looking into each other's
        eyes—
I staring up, you staring down—
    we both shudder, communing between your flexed legs, spread
    the width of my two shoulders: our four eyes,
        riveted in silence,
            agree! We have seen the bronze head nod. The eyelids
    flutter. The bronze bosom draw breath. The tarnished skins
        of metal wrinkling
            into folds over charcoal hid ribs. Organs—
            heart and lungs—of vegetable wax, waxen

liver, waxen pancreas. All glands,
    mercury, but in pure form, not poisons fed upon by dying
fish hordes. Our eyes swear we both saw
    bronze flesh breathe, bronze knees shift for comfort under all
    that obese weight (no gold in the fat buttocks, fat
        hips, we agree to that!),
            grand flab he can never jog off in throes
    of deep meditation. Does he diet, or fast?
        Does he shed bronze, gold,
            or weightless, sad wax only? We crane our necks
            to see how he leans and sways, as we wend

our wide, counterclockwise, happy circle
    around him, counting splendid curled petals of the great lotus-
blossom seat, the petals alternately
    pointing upward and curving downward, the puffed whirlwinds
    of incense smoke eddying up, thinning out,
        in sudden gusts and lulls,
            as if the blossom itself exhaled the perfume
    clouds submerging all but the Ancient's head, breath
        after vaporous breath . . .

We revolve, degree by slow degree, circling
the statue's base, half again wider

than the vast lotus throne half again
the diameter of the bloated God's girth, and we behold
the thousand views of the Buddha's
changing postures, the torso's bulk crafted by an army
of master sculptors. *Eight near-perfect castings*
in three years. Aborted casts,
unnumbered. No surmising how many dozens
of failed castings, cracked one-hundred-foot-wide
molds, collapsed scaffolds,
casters of irreplaceable genius crushed
in falling debris . . . Sudden glare!

We squint, sun cascading into the hall
from hidden windows high in the temple cupola—thousands
of sparkly points on the statue's
coruscating skull flare on, off, on, off, and I can see
great circles connecting all dots of light
on meticulously shaped
rondures of annealed jaw plates, shoulder plates, breast
plates, my sight traveling in arcs and swirls, curved
lines running in a mesh
of intersecting spirals dense as cross-
hatching in the divinely crafted

anatomies of Hieronymus Bosch
or the woodcut body dissections of Vesalius: God's
or human's, all the light-lines engraved
on the celestial body's grandly continuous surface
intersect. *Our body, a wing shining*
in the happy, happy
light of its wholeness. A moonlit angel's wing

in flight. Or underwater devil ray's
   wing torchlit
      by diver's forehead searchlight beam . . .
      High throne-back behind the Buddha's

head usurps our view while we wind
   around his back side, topped not by headrest or flat cushion,
as it had appeared to us wrongly
   in profile, but a goldleaf-covered broad wooden halo
   decorated with portraits of sixteen Bosatsu,
      by our ambulatory
         count, a troop of gilt sub-deities, satellites
      in orbit perpetually—each a mirror,
         or reflecting moon,
            to the one Daibutsu . . . *Oh, look! The whole halo*
            is shimmering, dancing before our eyes!

The Kofukuji Arsonists

In Kofukuji museum stands a phalanx
of august statues—stone, clay and bronze figures—
salvaged from two millennia of lordly
firebugs (can Japanese pyromania,
a dominant trait, be carried in the genes?) . . .

From era to era, embattled warlords
sped to be first to set fire to shrine or sacred
temple, each breathless to outpace the rival.
At midnight, all the sculpted deities, gathered
withindoors, relive their heroic couplings
to long-dead hermit priests who rescued them
throughout history, the monks keeping one jump
ahead of the royal incendiaries—
those feuding clans! Conflagrations erupt
like brushfires on a sun-baked hillside, each sparked

by insult or stain of honor. Yet always,
century after century, the exile
monk, life-taken-between-the-teeth outlaw
from both factions, steals into the blaze, leaps
through the circle of flames, and flying, wingless,

through the collapsing doorway, dodges falling
rafter, crumbling doorjamb—each a hoop of fire:
he must race flame-tongues licking across the walls,
sweeping interior chambers. A Kofukuji
student monk, trained in soldiership, always saves,
first, Kannon Bosatsu (the thousand-handed,
eleven-faced squatting Goddess of Mercy):
hoisting the statue, braced on the fireman's
carry-hold of his crossed forearms, or hefted
up high on his back; and then, tumbling backwards

through the flaming rubble, he drops to one knee,
perhaps, to dash out the sparks and swat away
white-hot embers that threaten to scorch her outer
skin—a shell of gold leaves, in a few spots the kiln-baked
gilt layer charring through, nearly exposing

the tougher second skin of japanned lacquer—
a hard black gloss of laminated varnish
miraculously resisting hottest coals,
the many-layered shellac epidermis
warding off demonic forked snake-tongues of flame . . .
He ignores the sizzling mouths of fire, open-
throated, gaping widely over his back
and flanks, soundless wails through the wounds of maws
in his scratchy haircloth shirt. He does not see
her thousand arms grow limber and soft, the frantic

waving of her hands brushing firebrands away
from all sides of his body as he flees: a few
dozen hands cupped and smothering the charred lips
of holes in his cloak; a few hands whisking the flamelets
(fingers of fire) away from his face and bare skull;

others, caressing and sheltering his singed—
but unfired—beard. Each of her eleven faces,
springing to life with a different expression,
assumes a guise to fortify his nerve
or ease his pain. He communes with the many-visaged
deity, taking strength from her glances—
smiles, grimaces, scowls, radiant beckonings . . .
He laughs outright, boldly gives thanks; then chides
his innocence, curses her for a Gorgon
in disguise—Medusa! He shuts his eyes, hurtles

through the smoldering egress, life, limb and saved
Goddess intact, barreling from the ash-heap
ruins . . . Sequestered in the outlying forest,
his laughter returns in a great timber-
splintering roar, irrepressible . . .

Flamingos of the Soda Lakes

They are standing, or stalking, in clouds—
          clouds of steam
welling up from the earth, vapors
     endlessly rising and fading to a thin mist:
     their bodies
are pink-white balls of smoke,
          clouds themselves,
ghostly feathered-eggs of solid
     cloud bobbing gently on jointed stilts,
     apparitional,
     great flocks of heavy smoke-ovals
          suspended in the upward-
thinning mists of smoke-haze . . .
     Thousands are waiting their turn to drink,
     thousands
squeezed into the tight circles
          surrounding thermal hot
springs studding Lake Hannington's shores,
     overflowing, and slowly draining into the lake;
     thousands
athirst and athirst, waiting
          to drop their long
snaking necks to the water to drink.
     The heads—flowers too heavy for their stems—
     loll
nervously over the always horizontal
          body-ovals. Now
the necks—those willowy S's—
     reversing their curves, swing the heads in a great
     semicircle
with a cranklike swiveling
          down to the boiling
shallows where they float, weightless,
     bobbing like buoys; and they swill great drafts

of fuming earth-
water through the leathery-soft petals
of their inverted bills.
As they drink they dance, they long-
leggedly skip and trot, leaping in steambaths,
a splendid
prancing on their arrowy stiff limbs,
hopping up and down,
teetering, shifting their top-heavy
weight lopsidedly from leg to leg-pole, never losing
their balance;
their necks undulating slowly, rhythmically,
adjusting the spoons
of their half-submerged upside-down bills
as they guzzle the boiling waters, keeping time
with their legs'
waltzing gait a-waggle from side to side,
while they shudder in exquisite
pain: whether more from the quaffed hot
rivers siphoning up their long necks and scalding
their throats,
or more from the fierce hot foamy effervescence
of the wading pools
that scorch their frail lower legs . . .
Now many are ruffling wingquills and little nubs
of tail-feathers,
warning rivals to make way and stand clear,
jealously guarding
their small dunking-and-dipping tracts;
and a few are butting each other with their flanks
and tufted rears,
jockeying closer and closer to the wellsprings,
where the fresh mineral
overflow waters from underground streams

seep up through the lakeshore mud; closer to the pure
    clear waters
of health, earth-filtered and effervescing,
        where the hissing sub-
terranean gases meet the clean open air,
    mixing their purities, cleansing over and over:
    refinings:
earth   air   water   light: where the sizzling
        earth-waters flow
into the fetid, brackish soda of the dense
    alkaline lake which, imbibed in large drafts, is noxious
    like seawater—
soda and salt, breeders of multitudes
        of unicellular life-
motes, poisons to higher forms: life-givers,
    life-takers.
             Flamingos, gladly suffering throat-burns,
    leg-burns,
suffering infernal hots for the pure, dance
        away the agonies
of hellfires for earth's life-elixirs,
    dancing for flames of wet that cannot singe a feather,
    dancing
to fill with firewater to satiety,
        to fill with flames
that cannot sear the long white angel
    plumes of their wings: a dancing to satiety—
    satieties
of thirstfire—a thirst dance!

Nara Park: Twilight Deer Feeding

Toward evening, sky's aqua
darkens to ultramarine,
strangely brighter over bald Mount Wakakusa
(treeless, dry grasses burnt in annual
January fête) than over wooded Mount Kasuga,
abode of the gods... We reenter these grounds—temple of the pagodas—
hurrying before sundown, before nightfall and the closing of gates,
bearing handfuls of small crackers
to offer the genial deer

one last, shy, long-nosed feeding.
We stroll in the deserted park,
dawdling. Are we sneak thieves? Or benefactors?
Why do we meander and leer behind?
It is twilight limbo. The deer, orbiting fitfully
in pairs all afternoon, now slink in passels of ten or twelve, or lurk
in shaded hedgerows. At our approach, they seem to dance sideways.
Or they float in sleep-languor,
neither toward nor away

from our glum coos and purrings
(now it is we who beg, not fawns
or does)... They move in weightless stupor,
a graceful bouncing on soft footpads
of paws, their just-lighter-than-air hindquarters
pitched to and fro, as if earth were sponge-turf on springs—flocks
of wingless, thin seraphim gliding across grassy cloud
scud, green cloudbanks of sod.
The children sidle up

to a lone deer—strayed a few feet
from its group; he backs away,
sweeping with a band of others to semi-seclusion

in a glen of cedars. No hideaway . . . The after-
glow of long-spent sunset, a pinkish tint on lawns
fading to lemon-sallow glimmerings, pastes a faint layer of luminous
glaze, momentarily, on all surfaces—embrace of the last light.
Halos of muted light, in enchanted
low-toned brilliance,

      encircle tree rinds, deer hides,
      shrines. Temple walls shimmer.
The sheen floods near and recedes in flashes,
light recoiling upon the beholder's eyes,
hypnotic—we blink, to no effect. The unearthly glow
dims, slowly fades into degrees of gray, the pinkish second skin
falling away, sliding off each surface . . . A cycle of toots,
high-pitched, eerie, pierces
the blanketing dusk!

      Horn-blasts from an unseen trumpeter.
      Scores of deer leap in unison,
springing from many quarters, well over a hundred
becoming visible at once. Emerging from the woods
in a full three-hundred-sixty-degree circle around us,
as if born spontaneously from the horn which summons them (punctual
daily signal), they converge upon a wisteria grove for sanctuary.
Following their course, the girls
try to intercept two

      frail stragglers, arms outstretched
      to enwrap each creature.
But the wiry featherweights, undeflected, with no
visible change in speed or direction,
slip past the puzzled children shaking their heads.
One fawn appears to pass, miragelike, through my stooping son's

hips and shoulder—in my sideview, a figure crosshatched,
   composed of shimmering diamonds
   and spheroids of light;

      in frontview, scrawnier and leggy,
         slim as an angelfish
      encountered, face to face, through underwater
   mask. The keeper, bugler of moments
   before, appears, waving a short flexible switch;
feebly snapping the whip, he herds some two-hundred-odd deer
into deep low pens . . . Instantaneously, scattered dots
   of light, mirrored on the surface
   of Sarusawa Pond,

      brighten! Whirling about-face, we witness
         a spectacle of colorful lanterns:
      well-lit octagonals and hexagonals, distributed
   everywhere in view, within or without
   the park. Of those nearest to us, half are stone lanterns
fastened to shrine walls, benches, or trelliswork. The other half, hung
aloft, metal lanterns suspended from roof eaves or oak limbs,
   sway gently in the breeze—rainbow
   phantasmagoria overhead!

Wreckage of the Pagoda Moons

(Kofukuji Temple, Nara)

Nothing moves
or murmurs but ourselves, as light
fails and fails—
all but an eerie shimmer
that comes and goes on shrine-walls and gravel path-
ways. Dusk thickens. Pools
and patches of shade merge in shadow—
unbroken dimness,
tans of oaken and cedar walls
deepening to sepias . . .
We circle the temple grounds, struck by absence, hush

of evacuation—
no stampede of gawky tourists
or prattle of guides.
Light winds enfold the deer park's
thousand wooded acres, relics and sacred pavilions
in quiescent chill, wrapping
the exquisite pagoda upper stories, square-
balconied, in mist . . .
Carla, thieving a last glimpse
of the turtle pond
behind her, bawls surprise. We all halt, turnabout.

A horizontal tower
stretches, in flattened repose,
to a recumbent length
double the height of its model,
or vertical too-solid twin: the five-storied pagoda
casting a long silhouette,
finely detailed black borders pasted
on starker white;
the midday showcase transformed

from a tub for scores
of tortoises, inching up and down the bank, to whitewash!

A moon-lit sheet
of fire . . . Hovering on the pool-edge,
we can see both
the iridescent sparkle of light
playing over shallow bottom-rocks and mirrored details
in the swan's-neck-sloping eaves
of the pagoda's profile. The moon, floating
beside the third level
tier, lights the balconies
of the near side etching
a lacy filigree, leaving the intricate far side roofs

eerily darkened . . .
Stunned, we turn from the standing
to the sleeping tower
and back, comparing. *No signals.*
By a shared impulse, unspoken, two daughters and father
bend for skipping stones to hurl,
and soon we are flinging one missile after another
at the towering monument
of shadow, our throws altering
from lateral tosses—
sidearm casts to induce flippity-flops over the surface—

to two-handed heaves
of larger rocks and boulders,
the playful glint
in our eyes varying to warriors'
glower: hurl by hurl, we work off our spleen
and funk born of the months
of difficult awe before all monuments, ceremony.

How much power we wield!
Power to shatter into splintering
fragments of light
the perfected icon of centuries. And power to dismantle

the moon's two-fold
replicas, the gleaming silver disk
pasted on the water's
dimmed creamy glaze. *Both moons.*
The twenty-one-carat-silver luminescent wafer.
The glistening tin alloy
overspreading the surface. *Both moons—mirror
and worn medallion—
fractured into shadow-light slivers
blended with the pagoda's
saw-edged chunks into the one blazing swirl of wreckage.*

FROM

Eros at the
World Kite Pageant

1983

Psychodrama: Tokyo Mime Film

Korean
Lady mime,
　　you suspend yourself beside the stunned
　　Caucasian seated
　　　　at table, waiting to order his meal,

his fate.
You will teach
　　him, wordlessly, about the void. Propped
　　on an invisible chair,
　　　　one leg crossed over the other, sipping

coffee,
your finger
　　curled in genteel crook around the handle
　　of a nonexistent
　　　　cup, you drop two missing lumps of sugar,

stirring
with a spoon
　　of air. He, pretending to ignore you—
　　secretly befuddled—
　　　　thinks he fears your sex, not guessing

the threat
is your one
　　possession: absence, the widening hole
　　in space torn by your id
　　　　turning itself inside out, eating

its way,
shadowily,
　　into everything solid around it . . .

Now you dance. You pirouette,
    spinning, weaving with your hands. You wrap him in

vacancy
and he cannot
    refuse it—it is his own silence you draw
    from him, strand by silken
        strand: a cocoon in which you wind and bind him.

Loves of the Peacocks

(Enoshima Zoo)

The sawdust-spattered plank floor is a stage:
        three small peahens drop
to their bellies at the erect bird's feet
      and cower, their wings incurled—a seamless blend
        with their shrinking posteriors.
      The male peafowl
opens and closes his iridescent wings,
        slowly, rising on his toes;
his chest swells, his wings a pump
      or bellows inflating his trunk and lengthy abdomen,
        by gradual puffs. We hear
      a faint hissing . . .
He squints his eyes, and swiftly unfolds
        the many loose webs
of his gorgeously elongated tail plumes
      into a broad half-moon-shaped aquamarine fan!—
        tripling the peafowl's height,
      a ten or twelve-
foot feather-span nearly filling the cage.
        His eyeslits appear
to close as scores of gold ocelli flash
      and shimmer, perhaps four or five eyespots spaced
        out over each long tail feather.
      Now the whole
tail shudders, the many eyes doubling,
        splitting into multiples
of gold flecks—thousands of unblinking irises
      stipple the ribbons of greeny iridescence fluttering
        from the base of each quill
      to the fork-tipped
feather ends . . .
        The three still hens, their plumage
        tucked under folded wings,

lie prostrate, softly clucking, entranced
by the prince's spell.
He is agitated, and his high
feather-tops start vibrating,
fiercely, like a row
of struck tuning forks while he turns and turns,
displaying front and rear:
in backview, he partly closes his tail,
as if to tease; tail widespread in frontview
(is he keeping time to music?)—
he pivots and struts,
again and again . . .
Eros or Narcissus, who is
his muse? I ask. *A courtship*
ritual, you reply,
A last pirouette!
Now dancing in place, he bobs up and down on tiptoe,
arching his broad cobra-hood
of tail forward
over the groveling peahens' heads; their long necks,
slithering from side
to side, scrape the gritty floor—scratch-sounds
blended with a chorus of low dull moans. Now the hens
contract their tails and wings
yet again,
as if trying to suck all of their appendages
back into the fetal torso-
hoop that budded them forth before birth,
and roll every stray feather into a perfect ball . . .
A volley of tremors, radiating
from the floor
planks, racks their prone bodies in waves:
each long shudder starts
with twitches and shakes of their undersides,

and the charge—overspreading their backs and necks—
flows upwards into arched pinions
of Apollo Cock
suspended above them (spreadwinged, he hovers
a few inches over the floor),
whose tail feathers, now brushing the cage-roof,
are given at last to such vigorous fluttering
they become an incandescent blur.
A halo arc.
Rainbow-hued. Rainbow-curved . . .
The shimmering border
highlights the many-webbed fan
of tail, which shades the croaking hens
nestled below, but illuminates the upper third
and outermost corners of stall:
flashing opal-
essence . . .
The colors keep changing, gold flares
winking on a blue-green backdrop,
white flares on orange, chartreuse on white:
now one color flames out, now another.
A brightest last flareup!
All lights
die at once. The many colors fade . . .
The cage—
it had doubled in size—is shrunk,
but the peahens, springing to their feet, win back
their full-feathered buxom physiques; while the grand
tail fan of the prince
had collapsed,
folded upon itself, shrivelling to less, less
than a shut accordion's flatness:
a moment's pinprick has punctured the swashbuckler's
glory-plumes, and he squats . . .

The hens,
cackling merrily, drive him
into a corner,
strutting and pecking his thin crown.
Next cage.
A second plumed Casanova
commences his display over a reclining cellmate.
Ah! Both heads wear crests
of upright tufts. *Plumelets.*
Which twin
is the wooer? I ask. *Which twin wooed?...*

The Tilemaker's Hill Fresco

I

The veteran tilesmith,
near his hut beneath the central bluff, cuts deep-dyed tiles
to shape. He salvages
the miscast odd pieces, molded wrongly
by kilns in his tileworks, that makeshift factory:
a few pre-fab steel girders
reinforced with concrete blocks and sealed with mortar;
walls on the north side only, the exposed frame
welcomes tenants—hawk or rodent . . . Assisted
by one skilled teenager,
he bakes thousands of fired-clay tablets daily. Together, they lift

the many glazed flat slabs
piled in neatly proportioned, truncated pyramids, stacked
high—but without a wobble—
in the two black wheelbarrows and rolled,
swiftly, to the tailgate of a fifties Ford pickup.
The two symmetrical heaps
of tiles are slid, intact, on a tough woven fabric, then
eased onto a mobile platform in the truck back—
a hydraulic jack?—which lifts or lowers
great bulks to the desired
level. The double load, transported across a steep upgrade

to a nearby hilltop
temple, is raised on the hydraulic device to a broad-based
scaffolding of ropes and boards.
The youth wrestles lines in the difficult
pulleys, while his mentor guides the plank framework:
now both tug the stage underfoot,
winding the combined weight of persons and two loads
of tiles, in slow—but constant—lift to eaves
of the curved high chapel roof. The self-

propelled escalator,
thin platform swinging in place, quits. They fasten the thick ropes,

swift hands weaving graceful
knots and loops, a classic ropecraft. *Tests knots. No slip-*
slack. Back-up knots, made fast
with snap of wrists. Fisherman's cast-reflex.
The tilemaster nods to his co-roofer. He spirals down
the dangling rope-end, unwound,
feeding through his two-fisted grip. *Rope-dancer!*
Or fireman sliding down ice-slick pole, who,
gaining speed as he nears the ground, brakes
just before impact. The man
on the roof crawls skyward, the load of tiles swelling his orange

back-pack: *buffalo's hump*
silhouetted against the bright cloud mass above him. His hill-
top roost far higher than ours,
we view him on an upslant: his stooped figure,
crablike, bordered by a shimmer of pinkish light, floats
across the roof's marked incline.
The master, too, looms above us, stretching to full height—
balanced, through shakily, on his truck-cab roof,
parked a short distance from the temple.
He surveys a dozen roofs,
all his own creations (the bounty of his thirty years' tenure—

by exclusive contract—
to the town), scattered, above and below, at graduated
and terraced intervals,
around and around the steep bluff, now topped
by the near-finished temple, appending its rich contour
of crosshatched dormers and gables
flowing between the pinnacle-spire and curled roof eaves

to the township's skyline. A bewitching sweep
of commingled roofs and hill-crests notch
Kashikojima Bay's
coast range . . . Is that weathercock, or true hawk, crowning the chapel's

spear-tipped steeple? I wonder . . .
Snuffed out. In a fleeting moment, erased. All outlines,
in this incisive clarity
of light, are clean-cut saliencies: Calder
sheet metal cutouts, hung from invisible thin wires
in a vast outdoors mobile—
improvised, say, to honor a Chicago Civic Center;
the artist concealed, hid behind his Cosmos
like the puppeteer lurking to one side
of marionette strings,
or the elegant tilesmith and roof-architect vanishing, today,

into anonymity
behind their roof tableau, while timber-and-tile highrise
sculptures convert to church,
residence, town hall, hospital, locomotives'
roundhouse, airship hangar and bus terminal . . . All roofs
take their place in the grand collage
of Japan's countrywide tile mosaic, a coast-to-coast
color kaleidoscope of the roofers' fine art.
Each town and city displays to bird's-eye
or airplane overview
its own uniquely sprawled horizontal roof fresco, shifting tilescapes

remodeled as lodgings fall
and are built again, fashioned by the accidental combined
hands of tilecraft genius . . .
Now the maestro, thirty-year-veteran,
stretches on tiptoe for the widest panoramic truck-top

vista of his rooftile fresco-
in-progress. He is waving his arms to the apprentice,
scolding directions, guiding the skilled handyman
on the roof through difficult crawls, hobbles:
sporting binoculars (twins
of *our* field glasses), he choreographs a dance of tile jugglery . . .

2

Impresario of the hill,
the happy tile-czar plots and maps out his roofdancer's
intricate moves. A pattern
unfolds. As the master prompts, so the protégé
lays tiles. Then, he breaks new ground: when he takes risks,
flouts rules, his eyes glow! Choices,
choices abound. Hazards of spacing, color arrangements,
placement of off-shade tiles of varied shapes
and odd sizes: triangles, diamonds, ellipses,
rhomboids, squares perhaps—
he rejects false settings, color match-ups that do not ring true

for his keen tilist eye.
He selects—in the speedy flux of options—happiest
blends and designs. Journeyman
and fledgling, bowed to his knees, he still tracks
signals from his tutor by taking quick sidelong glimpses—
ah, slowly he creeps into his roof-
walker's second skin of an artist!
The coach on the truck-top
devises a code as diverse (to our untutored
eyes) as semaphore alphabets—if delivered
flagless, batonless. *Forearm*
hand chops. Airbursts of cupped-hand poppings in underarms. Curled tongue

clickety clacks. Forehead thwacks.
   Castanetlike finger-snappings . . .
                              Light shifts. The tilemaster,
      elongated in stark relief
      against the hillside backdrop, casts a long shadow
      which seems to quiver, magically, in the lusterless sheen
   of the late dull sun. The shadow,
undulant, wavers from side to side, flickering upon walls
of three or four of the nearby buildings, all roofed
by his own tile handiwork over the years.
         His shadow fluctuates, now,
in rhythm with the encroaching dusk wind's soft hands giving caress

         to the flat cedar sidings
      and broad wall panels. So intensely does he behold (his eye
      a camera's wideangled lens),
      he takes in a one-hundred-eighty-degree expanse,
      a topography of roofs mantling the hill, at all levels
   from summit to ground zero . . .
We sense the pace of teamwork quickens, accelerates, both men
racing the fall of the sun, and the last good light
does seem to falter, to stall, as if secretly
         befriending their labors
(oh, beauteous enterprise!) . . .
                     It may be, the master exults: a trance

         steals over his features,
      while he scans the exquisite geometries of his hillslope
      mosaic nearing completion.
   The bluff looks subdivided, carved by late shadows
   and oblique slants of light into three wide tall panels
of a vast outdoors triptych
facing to east, north, and west. He rotates his binoculars,
slowly, from side to side, bowing his head in homage,

thrice, to each phantasmal scarp of tile-roofed
                    declivity. Each roofshelf,
a distinct plane of hillscape, expresses—in its pattern of shuffled

                    blocks, plates, and flat oblongs
              of color stacked like bright dominoes in sloped-roof chains—
              a range of tones to match Nature
              herself. The scene beheld offers to our eyes
              a new calculus for decoding Planet Earth's minute lush
              particularity, which,
          if viewed by a Paul Cézanne, say, could reveal—in a flash—
          a first Incarnate Alphabet for Cubist art . . .
Taking turns with *our* glasses, we oscillate
                    between tiers of tile layouts—
unevenly spaced, at many sites of hillside—and rainbow terraces

                    of nearby flower gardens
              fashioned by local experts in *ikebana,* arrangements
              of azaleas, peonies, irises,
              camellias and morning glories, clustered
              in bright patches on the hillface—zoned in geometric
              segments: long narrow rectangles,
          wide ellipses, isosceles triangles, squares, trapezoids,
          each a rioting cornucopia of color
      mirroring the palette (limitless
                    shades, tones, hues, nuances)
of adjacent tile displays. Here, the tranced viewer grasps images

                    of the seen world as a flux
              of intersecting cones, rotating cylinders, pyramids, cubes
              and spheres. All living parts
          of *this* landscape, to be deciphered by human eyes,
          must be apprehended as a pattern of colors and shapes
      molded by joint artistries

of the *ikebana* horticulturist and rooftile architect
(the two cultures, with unearthly charm, nourish
each other, casting a double spell
on haunted witnesses):
the Eye, thus illumined, dissects Nature into a mesh, webwork

of geometric solids,
whirling like pinwheels or weathervanes in juxtaposed orbits.
Sight, itself, takes the form
of so many diamonds and spheroids, revolving
in the perfect balance of gyroscopes, planets, asteroids!
They are both the scene beheld
and the Eye's imitation of it. The myriad-flecked
tile-and-flower show and the act of seeing
are One. Cubism. Not a concocted pose,
dogma of elitist few
savants, but true faculty shared by the Eye and all things sighted.

3

I fancy the tilemaster
in his youth—devotee of Cézanne's landscapes, his passion
burgeoning throughout six years
of study and travel in France. Today, finding
in terrains of his homeland prototypes for the exalted
hidden orders rendered
luminous, as by fluoroscopy, in Cézanne's great cliff-scarps
in oils, he sets out to electrify for common eyes
(and ours!) the extraterrestrial beauty
of unseen geographies
lurking within many a haunted landscape. This seaside bluff is the last

tableau of his secret career
in alchemy, his mission as translator of the actual earth,

terrestrium on the city's
outskirts, into its ideal other form: *divine roof-
symmetries!* . . . By following a mathematics of tile layouts
wedding Nature to homecrafts,
a celestial earth dweller's art, he does honor to both
Pythagoras' "Music of the Spheres" and Lucretius'
De Rerum Natura, but taking Cézanne
as his patron Saint . . .
Now he infuses into body language of his delivery hand-wafts

of dance choreographer,
lilted gestures of band conductor on his podium, or opera
scenarist molding stage sets
(he has studied their styles in theatre rehearsals) . . .
So it is he waves commands to his apprentice and heir,
the disciple who may carry
into the future this rare exterior decorator's genre
of landscapist high art . . .
The low ochre sun,
passing behind a slow cloud, reemerges,
darkening to wine-amber
as it nears the horizon. All the petal-and-tile bouquets take on

shades of crimson, lowest tiers
incarnadined, the highest cloud-pale pinks. The men, as before,
quicken their to-and-fro signals
and tile settings. The master *is* Cézanne, his canvas
the many-layered sweep of hillslopes. They rage to finish
two small dormer roofs by dark,
cupolas perched, mosquelike, on opposite sides of the base roof
serving as floor to the two miniature domes. The tilists,
wearied, have saved for last, for day's end,
these exact twin replicas
of the temple structure below, models of the original church

fashioned to the smaller scale
in all particulars, two whole tiny chapels atop the parent
tabernacle . . .
                    The tall youth,
stretching to his full lanky height, reaches upwards
from the lower roof, a steeplejack on his tower stacking
tiles in immaculate rows,
then anchoring them in place with steel rivets. Working in clockwise
circles around each dwarf roof, in turn, he slams the barrel
of his rivet gun into roofboards, vibrating
                    the whole midget cabin
in his fury, taking fire from his senior co-aerialist, each balanced

                    on his flat roof trapeze:
the one waltzing in circles, around and around a temple top
of cracked planks and shaky rafters
(saved by the stout cedar king posts and ridgepole);
the other stomping up and down, bobbing on the rust-eaten
truck roof below, partway caved-in
on the rearward side, tattered upholstery showing through gaps
in the metal. Now the superior is waving his arms,
gesticulating in a final passion: last
                    block-outs of the design
and color match-ups. No time left to correct mistakes, all last choices

                    of chromatic blends and tile-
fittings are blurted out in a flash of sudden insights, a blaze
of second-seeing, as day's light
slowly fails . . .
                         Though the air is still (no leaf or petal
flickers), all garden plots and roofs break up before his eyes!
The separate roof tiles and blooms
lose their outlines—their natural borders, edges, surfaces
and skins blurring. The inner substances, or mass,
spills out of its casings. All things living,

or non-living, transgress
the limits set by orders of chemistry and physics. Thus, the atoms

and molecular bondings
of each flower species; the compounds of each scent, fragrance;
the meshwork of electrons
in each element of metals, rocks, earth clods, seabrine
and mountain streams—all are breaking up in the cyclotron
of the artist's piercing vision.
Laser beams or high-speeding supersonic neutrons of second sight
bombard all things, exploding their atomic make-up,
dissolving their nature, a Second Nature
welling up from wreckage,
the ruins of matter. A new order, phoenixlike, is born from debris.

All souls of flower, rock, soil,
timber, flint, glass, tile—come back as galaxies of perfectly
formed geometric bodies,
symmetrical as snowflakes, spinning in fixed planes
or circling in three-dimensional orbits. Cézanne's spheres,
cubes, and intersecting ellipsoids
project, for the viewer, an order of stable identities.
A mathematics that endures (oh, steadfast cosmos!),
and survives—like inner light—the withering
of vines, stems, limbs to dust . . .
The incinerating of walls, floors, roofs to ash . . . Our collapse of bodies . . .

Eros at the World Kite Pageant

(Santiago, Dominican Republic)

Our host, Don Tomás Morel—retired mayor,
　poet, folklorist—slips off
　　into nostalgias . . . He takes us back
　　　fifteen years
　　　to the earliest days
　of his seclusion—
the withdrawal from public
office, his shy first trials and delights
as amateur folklorist,
　　　the slow nurturing of his zeal
　to revive the lost communal folk arts—fad
　　of his youth . . . Ah, he begins
　　with kites. First, a scholar, he researches

　　　the origins of kitecraft
　in ancient tribes, poring over old sketches,
　　　rudimentary drawings
　of virtuoso kites;
　　　then, he molds large block
　　　　prints portraying fantasy kites
　　　in designs that recall Marc Chagall's dream flights,
　　　and runs off hundreds of colorful posters
　highlighting the date, place, and prizes
　to be awarded in the first worldwide kite contest . . .
Each week, for two months,
　　drafting new kite models, he dispatches
　　couriers to all seaside cities, mountain or backwoods
towns, to hang the posters on all prominent
billboards, roadside barns,

and farmers' markets—promoting the all-star
　kite Olympiad. He sponsors

bi-weekly ads on radio and TV
news broadcasts
for all the world as if kite-
flying pageants,
or tourneys, are as common
as annual lotteries, beauty queen contests,
or cockfights . . . The weekend
of kitefest, whole townships come
to Santiago from all parishes of the country
in caravans mixing ox-carts,
motorbikes, schoolbuses, horsemen, firetrucks,

twenty-wheel semi oil rigs,
chauffeur-driven Rolls limos, two-cylinder
electric cars—record traffic
jams on all main roads
into town, many families
pitching tents and slinging hammocks
between trees eight to ten miles outside the city
limits (to avoid the "criminal riffraff") . . .
At daybreak, a full hour before sunrise,
hundreds of men and boys assemble at the foot
of the one hogback-
humped broad high hill in town, topped
by Trujillo's columnar tower—one of many monuments
scattered about the country his worship erected
to commemorate himself

in a race, perhaps, with his own assassin.
Most kite-makers tote two
or more kites, cradled away from raw wind-
chops, the delicate
glossy papers and silks tied
to featherweight

thin sticks of balsam: all kites
are wrapped in bed sheets or heavy-gauge plastic
    (so like prize fighting-cocks
        shaded under hoods and carried
    to the bout in cages) . . . Each lone kitist climbs
        to his appointed hillside
        terrace. The three or four dozen acres

        of grassy slopes encircling
        the monument are subdivided and parceled out
            to all registered entrants,
        while the plateau
            on the hill's far side—
            a treeless expanse groomed and trimmed
            yearlong as a polo grounds—is reserved for hundreds
                of teenage and child kitists, who are allotted
        half-hour shifts, from first light to dusk.
        Today, even the "Capuchin," the tiny-to-small kites
    of the children, are dubbed—
    with strict formality—*flying artifacts.*
        But early on, the kids may be seen racing to and fro,
    crisscrossing, tripping over each other's lines,
    falling and laughing

and colliding with their fellows, from one end
    of the polo courts to the other.
        One child, ignoring the shouts and appeals
            of thousands
            in the clumped galleries
        of spectators,
        continues to chase a runaway
    kite trailing a swiftly unwound ball of string,
        his legs entangled
            in three or four lines issuing

from opposite directions—now dragging two dropped
and bedraggled spools of twine,
as well as the downed kite of a comrade

twisting and shredding on the turf
in his wake. Another tall kite, descending, swoops
onto his back like a vulture,
its upper brace of crossed
sticks clinging to his shoulder,
two strips of white sheeting dangled
from his spine as he runs, a white devil's forked tail . . .
The two judges in pursuit are retired police
sergeants: one thick-necked and hippy,
the other preceded by a colossal triple chin
billowing into tight-
belted double paunch, the latter resembling
an upright camel's twin humps. As if he carries sacks
of molasses, his multiple jelly rolls of flesh—
bouncing up and down

as he runs—keep up their own unique tempo
of jiggles and jolts, queerly
at odds with the rhythm of his galloping legs
and erect frame.
Red-faced, he bellows threats
at the fugitive:
"Rule-breaker, you're disqualified!
Halt! Pay the fines," all lost on those runaway
urchin ears. But most infant
kite-flyers abide by the rules,
staying within the time limits and narrow borders
of their allotted purlieu
on the polo turf. The nearsighted, half-deaf

judges, milling around the junior
contestants, mark points on their bulky pasteboard
    scorecards, catching kite-tails
and snagging slack lines
    in their stiff formal uniforms,
        defaulting more often than any child:
        they back into each other, signposts, and out-of-bounds
        markers, as they weave in and out of the ranks
of four or five youth divisions
bunched, by age increments, in far corners of the field . . .
One skilled operator,
    juggling two kites of Punch and Judy—
    one set of strings in each hand—employs a precise code
of finger controls, giving to the airborne
hero and heroine

animated and sprightly stick-figure moves
    of marionettes. All limbs
        and face parts (lower jaw, ears and nose)
            wag, or gesture,
            independently in the vivid
        sky pantomime,
        both puppet figures launched
into sudden jumps, dives, side-leaps and bouts
    in the celebrated
        love-spat battles of the sexes.
    The slaps and falls are tautly measured, despite gusts
        and sudden shifts in wind direction,
        the wind a quick-change artist in its own right

        matched, swerve for swerve, by this child
    prodigy puppeteer . . . The fans and other performers,
        diverted from their antics,
    are swept away

by the mime show's last act,
     a spellbinder! Punch clobbers Judy
into a terrific nosedive and tailspin. He zooms
     after her in pursuit, overtakes her plunge
but—unable to stop—Punch hurtles
     toward earth, his pointy nose aimed at a mesmerized chaplain-
judge's unprotected
     bald pate. Ah, it's Judy who loops,
     at the last, and breaks Punch's deadfall, catching him
in a fluttery kite-twinning hug and kiss,
the two figures sailing off

in separate leisurely ascents . . . No one doubts
  the verdict: winner of the Junior
     League first prize. The senior competition gets off
     to a slow start,
     many distinguished entrants
     arriving late, drunk;
  the main events in full swing by mid-
afternoon, perhaps eight hundred of the expected
  two thousand artifacts
     in the "Chichigua" (maxikites)
     division crowding the lower heavens with dense kite
        galaxies and constellations,
        amazingly few sideswipes, tangles, or snarls,

        in view of the congested
     sky field. At peak overcrowding, swarms of kites
        of all sizes and shapes
     dodge each other
        in high winds, the flat kites
           limited to diagonal and up-down
           trajectories, a few tall box-kites spiralling
              and looping in horizontal orbits . . .

148

Someone exclaims, Trujillo's monument
should be employed—by judges who are not half-blind—
as an airport watchtower,
controllers allocating the throngs
of airtraffic to restricted sky lanes ... Now the veteran
kite-flyers, leaping hurdles, migrate up and down
the various strata

of hillside, swiftly traversing the short arcs
    of Government Hill's perimeter
        ascribed to their maneuvers. They keep seeking
            better vantage
            to display their aerial stunts
        and handicraft
        to the audience and judges,
    alike, thousands of spectators merging in clusters,
        here and there, at the hill's
            foot (the viewers roped off from rugged
            hillslopes, reserved for kite pilots) ... When a new star
            brightens the firmament of kites,
            news travels fast through the clumped masses,

            and a great surge of thousands—
        leaving a few lost stragglers all but trampled
            underfoot in the wake
        of the stampede—
            sweeps to the rumored site, to get
                close-up views of particular marvels ...
            The flying *El Presidente* beerbottle starts to sputter!
                Its top blows off with a great pop, an explosion
        of many fireworks at once—the smoke
        billows gushing from the bottleneck simulate the head
    on a fizzly giant glass
        of beer ... No sooner do the vast wings

of the crowd on the hill's east side converge into one
shouting and swaying and heaving crush of fans,
the next aerial highlight—

punctual as Halley's Comet—flares into view
   at a remote edge of the skyfair
      arena, and a whirling vortex of onlookers
         is swept, helplessly,
            into the ideal observatory
         site (as tens
      of thousands of iron filings
are drawn from all sides to a powerful magnet
   suddenly dropped in their midst);
         and now, they charge around the plaza
      to the hill's north end to view, in succession,
         a three-ring-circus staged
            by gifted brothers of the same family

         team, whose renowned surname
      is linked, in memory, to record-setting feats
   in many popular sports.
      The spirit invoked
         in the gallery recalls
            blood lust of devotees for a family
         of trapeze artists who perform daredevil stunts
            without a net. The first wields a box-kite
   modeled after a flying cigarette
carton with his left hand, a tall vertical-box lighter
balanced from his right wrist.
      The two boxes float toward each other
   at a height of one hundred meters. The wide carton
box-top flies open—a white giant cigarette
pops out, the lighter top

snapping open at the same instant. A fireworks
   display erupts from the latter,
      igniting the white tip of the giant
         tobacco stick,
            suspended in flight—invisibly—
   by its own guideline.
The lit end of the mock cigarette
glows with a dull pinkish gleam (barely sighted
   on the bright sunny backdrop);
      and the slow-burn ember travels,
         by eerie gradual shifts, from one end of the poised
            unmoving white cylinder
            to the other, leaving a scroll of dark ash

            in its place, which disintegrates—
         all at once—into a spray of grey confetti mixed
            with fading sparkles.
The second brother
      launches a tall pleated kite,
         much wider at the top than the bottom.
      The many vertical folds, creases running lengthwise,
         resemble a closed accordion's deflated
   wind bag. Ah, the pleats commence to open!
   The crowd sucks in its breath and gasps, as if they expect—
at any moment—a few chords
   of arpeggios and musical scales
   will come raining down into their ears, a kite concert
of the skies (a fantasy not unlike cartoon angels,
hidden in clouds, plucking

the strings of their small beneficent harps);
   and they avert their eyes from kite
      to wizard, unwilling to let his tricks or sleights
         escape their sight,

braced for him to perform feats
as a long-distance
accordionist. But when they look
again, no music ventriloquism is in progress.
      They behold a giant fan
            opening and closing in the sky,
         much as living sea fans are observed to blossom,
         unblossom, in close-ups
         of underwater films shot from a bathysphere

            in Jacques Cousteau sea odysseys . . .
      So allured is the audience by the kite-fan's motions,
            bellowslike—its puffed sides
      breathing in and out
            like angels' lungs—they overlook
                  the nimble machinations of brother
                  number three, who levitates three oddly compressed kites
                  at once. Vaguely female, they resemble
         floppy deflated clothes mannikins.
         Not until the trio of shapeless scrawny-bird sisters
      rises to a level
            some yards below the respiratory fan
            spreading *its* unfolded wing plumes wider and wider—
      hypnotic!—do the multitude of viewers lower
      their eyes to discover

three dilapidated uprisen women, their flattened
   skin bags starting to fill out,
      swelling faster and faster, while a steady hiss
         (a sound like air
         escaping from a just-punctured
      bike tire going flat:
      or the sound of a manned fleet
   of hot-air balloons passing overhead, a hissing

to drive tame household dogs
    rabid with unstoppable yelping)
  becomes audible to all stationed directly below,
    and to many a short radius
    removed from that bombsight zero precinct . . .

     The prolonged hiss climaxes
   in a few soft pops, firecracker reports or cap
     pistol shots. By abrupt shifts,
   almost too quick
      for the unaided eye to follow,
        the drooped figures puff into shapely
        dolls, and next, mellow into living dolls kicking
         a cancan (those few blessed with field
   glasses, or binoculars, catch nuances
   of the sudden anatomical switch, the swift two-step
  metamorphoses missed
    by the others) . . . The familiar fan,
    above, drops, partially hiding the dancing girls,
the chorus flirting and teasing the viewers
with glimpses of their buxom

cleavage and dimpled thighs, while the broad fan
  alternately exposes and shields
    their sexual glamours, as it opens and closes—
    a chastity guard?—
    in front of the chorus line.
  The wideopen fan
  spans all three beauties
executing their bows, kick-ups and pirouettes
  in perfect formation, half-
     veiled behind their modesty screen
    (the two brothers coordinating the four puppet
     kites with uncanny true-to-life

spark and verve); the eyes of beholders

    glazed with lust only flesh-
    and-blood disco lovelies or go-go twisters
    should arouse. The sober
ecclesiastics
       (divested of all priestly
         garb, doubling as umpires), titillated
         themselves, are willing to pass over lesser deviltries,
          not fooled by the fandancers' screen.
    But their dander is piqued by outright
    sodomy—for now, blinding sight, slinking down low, lower,
  behind the outspread fan
    taking the shape, at last, of a full semi-
    circle, the viewers can guess the lewd acts simulated
by two reclining figures: the prone chorus girl
humping her supine mate, upswung

legs of the latter reversed, the stroking feet
  of both partners to the supposed act
    visible beyond the rim of the half-moon fan . . .
    The third figure,
    hanging back, tosses her head
  backward and forward,
    though she faces her coupled
and fornicating chums. Now crouching on her hands
  and knees, she passes
      one hand to and fro between her legs
    faster and faster, stopped by howls from the two
    clergymen referees: "For shame!"
    "Foul! Foul!—disqualified . . . " Louder pops.

    Three beauty queens shrivel,
    collapsed in their quick-shrunk hides. The prank backfires.

Thus, the clear-cut Grand Prize winners,
top-flight family
      talents, are ousted from the weekend
         Olympiad . . . Three hours to the box-kite
      adult tourneys. Four hours to the bird kites. All winners
         chosen by judges' ballots, the awards given.
The last day's tryouts and contest fêted
by an allout pig and lamb slaughter, followed by allnight
barbecue: whole carcasses
      buried, baked in beds of white-hot coals;
      whole tunas and jewfish flung into the pits, atop the swine:
a fresh-caught gift, gratis, to outland visitors
from the local fisherfolk . . .

Moonlighters

Too late for the westend sunset,
stalled on a flat-topped
bluff for hours:
three microbuses
of our caravan parked
at odd angles, we straddle road
and grassy shoulder ... Our three
drivers—two Carib Blacks, one East
Indian—squat
beside an aged, tall
pimento tree
(past fruitbearing; bark scrolling off
in long peels; fragrant of allspice, tangy) ...

They whittle and sand small blocks
and twists of wood into
artifacts,
primitive heads and busts.
Our troop of twenty,
enticed by chanted palaver,
are trapped by a sales force
of dozens, all classes and ages
wielding a sales pitch—
from nonagenarians
to urchins.
The six-year-old oval-faced charmer,
in bermudas, waves colorful cacao bean

necklaces under our flared nostrils,
so freshly picked we whiff
the tart scents
of hacked-open pods ...
Men and boys, cane pickers
and huskers, jobless truckers, bauxite

miners and haulers—moonlighters,
one and all! Handicraft experts,
carvers and whittlers,
they offer cut-rate prices
for Afro heads.
Craggy, wide foreheads. Deep pouches
under eyes. Long sinuous indented ears,

orchidshaped. Carved from coconuts, chunks
of soft cottonwood, guano.
Small handsized
figurines. Totem
pole heads, elongated,
many faces stacked in rows, one
atop the other. Heavy block-
wood sculptures for the mantelpiece.
Basic prototypes—
mythic scowl or dreamy trance—
are repeated
in all sizes. The few artists add
bold flourish to lip or pendulous earlobes . . .

A teenage boy hands a many-branched
candelabralike limb
through the van
window—we pass the prize
back and forth, driftwood twists
blended with handprint whorl patterns
of the grain (genius in shape
and polishing), the successive branch forks
grafted on all sides
spiralling up the yard-long
stalk, each stem

capped by a removable carved swallow,
thrush, or grackle. The birds, anchored to thin

shafts, are slid in and out of the trunk.
Wide-eyed! That arch of neck
and cast of beak
so lifelike, I expect
wings to flutter, unfurl; tails
to shudder in flight from the hands
of tourists sampling wares,
then fitting the birds back in their sockets
like so many candles
inserted in candelabrum
cups. One branch tip,
someone scolds, is blunted, splintered.
A haggling over prices! This true virtuoso

wood sculpture—marred by one *un*perfect
edge—drops, drops in price
while Voodoo
and Obeah busts command
outsize fees . . . A shuffling of sandaled
feet. The oldest merchant, face
shrunk and furrowed like a prune or fig,
prances in front of a small child
parading necklaces.
He, inches shorter, stunted
and hoop-backed,
struts from side to side, a hop-and-skip
dance step, strumming a makeshift wee violin:

an eight-inch hollow bamboo segment
carved to a miniature
fiddle shape,

the bow a slim turkey
bone wand swept to and fro
across three mounted dental floss strings.
He squeaks forth his repertoire
of catchy tunes, keeping up
a vervy beat. Note-
flawless! *Home on the Range.*
Oh! Susanna.
Old Belafonte calypso hymns. He sells—
crowd humming along—two dozen bows, fiddles . . .

Saltcod Red

Curled red locks looped back over the shoe-sole parabola
bald strip indenting your scalp, and fanning out in a bulb

in back; thick cockney accent; eye wrinkles more deeply furrowed
on the left side, left cheek always lifted for the chuckles

or chronic bursts of laughter—your happiest trait—that threads
in and out of your story-telling gabble; fine figure

of a tall man, still the *impress* cut by your lordly swagger
despite round-shouldered stoop and swaybacked cave-in of spine

(lordosis on one side twinned by paunch on the other) ... You muse
upon the years lost in Foreign Service in the Veldt, worse

in the African Bush—you *bore* your malarial fevers
(no water for days at a stretch), while others in the camp

sank into coma, weekly, you left with seasonal joint aches,
arthritic twinges—no more; and now, even as I whine

my paranoid asides, terrified of machete-armed
Jamaican muggers hiding behind each rock or shrub, you bolt

erect! You add three inches to your six foot sag-frame,
anterior and posterior S-curves flattened into Youth's

ramrod physique reemergent ("No thieving riffraff will dare
to hit on *us!*"), these weeks a well-earned respite from bonanza

years in fresh-frozen fish, back home in frigid Montreal.
Little do the native islanders guess your company

exports tons of Canada saltcod which, coupled with local
ackee redfruit, makes up the favorite national food:

SALTFISH & ACKEE a native emblem displayed in all diners
and speakeasies, alike. I grin at all jokes heard, jokes unheard;

I must see your profile, half-read those lips to decipher
your rich brogue (lampoonings of all local foibles) . . . Too shy

to beg you to repeat punch lines, I'm happy to catch tuneful
song lyrics of your badinage if I miss the sly words . . .

FROM

The Mural
of Wakeful Sleep

1985

Many things are first appearances... places only briefly visited → are from real life or mostly so...

pictures ....grow into his language

The Banana Dwarf

I turn the market corner, then peer down
the busiest Santo
Domingo
central thoroughfare,
sidewalk traffic as thronged
with surplus foot peddlers and shoppers
as the vehicular jam-up
on the mainstreet intersection. The number
of side-by-side lanes,
in road *or* walkway, varies
from three to ten:
pedestrians, buglike motorcarts, bikes
and cabs whirl and slither around each other,

weave in and out of formation, like couples
on a disco-clogged
dance floor ...
At a city block corner,
three roads distant, I see—
gliding swiftly through a thick huddle of heads
and shoulders—a whirring machine!
Is it a crane, two blurred yellow derrick beams
swung on each side
of the advancing figure
or apparatus—
but not mowing down the crush of bodies
it plows across? The heads bob this way and that,

steering clear of those thick yellow posts
hoisting burdens, two
on each side,
revealed to be tall stalks
of bananas—a pair suspended
from each long wooden pole. The banana dwarf

165

takes springy strides, so much bounce
in pads of his moccasins, he matches a gymnast
on a trampoline;
for length and limber play,
his transverse rods
resemble pole vaulters' posts. Amazingly,
no single bananas fly loose—the ripest clusters,

even, stay intact—his difficult balancement
both dance step and juggler's
lofty art.
This spry, red-cheeked midget
looms tall, tall—and oh!—still taller
for the yellow tiered forest of fruit he wields
with his graceful plump shoulders,
his back and neck muscles rippling. The taut fruit
of his flesh: cords
and sinews, sleek flexors bunched
under his skin—
bananas themselves—bulge the human rind
of his upper torso . . . He sways nearer and nearer.

Though I walk jauntily toward him, I seem
to stand still, to hang
in a pool
of banana fluff, banana
yellow light emitted from the stalks:
a cloud, in which I float, weightless, tongueless,
wanting to speak—to beg a choice
ripe banana to eat. *He flies. He sings the all-*
saving nutrients,
blessings of the Banana
God. He plucks

a sample banana here, a sample there, peels
one, offers a munch to each of several passersby,

    drops a pinch of banana in my outstretched
        palm. *His bare chest, shoulders,*
              shed their skins.
        That ripply musculature,
     bared and exposed, offers itself up
  to the eyes of one and all, to the great yellow
   Eye of the Banana Lord, Sun.
And when he glides behind me, my Dominican
        pesos flicker
      like a new papery tongue
       between his teeth,
the extra money bisecting his widest smile,
a nine-banana spiral draped over my wrist, the coil

    and whorl of the golden cluster symmetrical
      as a pineapple, my small vine-
        twist of fruit
      wee replica of the many-tiered,
   many-wreathed stalks of banana garlands
slung from the Banana Apostle's shoulders . . . All those
    he passes—ladies of wide girth,
men of tall stature, children—must duck, weave, swerve,
       but not one Soul
    collides with a single gold
      shaft! Their moves
guided by his hops, they dodge banana flower-burst,
their dance in traffic as deft as his fleet pirouettes.

[handwritten margin annotation: ← Lost stanza starts here (except for interjection)]

Siesta

No rustle.
   Not a lip
      stirs in the town square,
      the park frozen
in mid-Siesta . . . The horse-drawn buggies
are parked in roadside stalls, their drivers curled
      in front seat corners
      like snails; long horse necks drooped

between traces,
    in stupor, or
      quiet munchings of hay.
    Thick manes wag
in the breeze, while snuffles punctuate
the masters' snores: a mixed chorus of sleep drone
      and gap-toothed slow hay
      mastications . . . The buses, fire engines,

ambulancias,
    and tractors—
      all parked at odd angles—
      straddle lanes
half-on, half-off the highway. Dormant
at the foot of park statues (military sculptures:
      pistols aimed, swords
      drawn, or crouched beside cannons),

the hodgepodge
    fleet of trucks lies
      sprawled. They strike poses
      of slain dragons
or disabled war tanks: front or rear axle
swung over low hedge, one wheel propped on high curb,

or athwart boulder;
whole garbage truck-back chassis

atilt. Cement
 truck's bumper
  near-submerged in the park
  fountain. Loaded
banana trailer and sugar-cane trailer
sandwich the cab of giant diesel semi (its three-
  story-high fortress
  towering over the sunburst

cornucopias
 of fruit and cane),
  dislodged from its massive
  chrome-silver
torpedo: close facsimile of an Inter-
Continental Ballistic Missile! The twenty-four-wheel
  oil rig tanker
  floats in a field opposite

the plaza square . . .
 Many drivers' doors—
  above, below—slant ajar:
  a few doors,
swiveling on their hinges, gently sway
in the wind; others anchored by legs poking upwards
  through windows, feet
  shoeless, sock-bedraggled or bare . . .

The Organist's Black Carnation

Odd music,
cutting through horn blasts and squawks of traffic, asserts
    its live and public wash
of sound rolling in waves across the town square . . . Christ Church
Cathedral. Once in the Church rear courtyard, we find
we can disencumber the river of organ song from percussive
    street blare—
    its source, the deep hall within tall double doors,
        unbolted. Mother
                and I, goose-stepping
on circular, wide ceramic tiles of the walkway, traverse
    the Church
gardens, and pass through the side entrance. The instrument,
    itself, so near the door, we almost collide
with the seated performer, his arms and legs all pumping
    together, the four limbs
utterly weightless, his moves between upper and lower keyboards
effortless, unwilled,

as buoyed up
by a hidden well of pure feeling as his side-to-side runs
    across any one keyboard.
    Tall. Blond. Bearded. American. Stops to turn pages. Smiles
    Hello. *Any music you prefer,* he asks? *Oh yes,*
any Bach. Bach Preludes unfold, at once—the music open
    before him.
    But he could be playing from memory. Or sightreading.
    A little of each,
                I'd guess, never up close
to an organist expert before, I gasp at agilities
    of legwork,
the sheer quantity of wooden pedals, joined in a concave arc
    recessed below his legs, his knees spreading wide,
wider, as he reaches for the pedals at either far end—

there are so many
moving parts, keys and pedals above and below, I can see, at last,
why organ solo

music I've heard
can sound like a whole orchestra of virtuosos. How lightly
        he taps the keys, oceans
    of rich basses circulating around the whole chapel, cloister,
        and outer chambers—the tall pipes widely distributed
    throughout the walls, as if the entire church is the vehicle
        and body
    of the instrument, the keyboards and pedal valves
        a mere touch control
                        relay . . . Organ melody
    outside the church, diffused, half-muffled by traffic,
        is carried
afar, and, for moments, rushes close to the distant listener's
        ears; but withindoors, the whole church interior
is charged with the music's amplified wave pulsings, notes
        that seem to pass beyond
all time limits, as in Bruckner's symphonies. It's all a breathing,
influx and efflux

of lungs shaped
like tall pipes, the wide oval pipe tops releasing blent voices,
        four voice octaves rolled
    into the one chorale . . . He chats with us now as he plays, simpler
        passages he *must* know from memory. Keeps turning pages,
    though. No mistakes. His movements all dancelike. I look and look,
        scrutinize
    his hands, the faraway pipes, for clues to the miracle
        of lightness of touch—
                      so feathery his patter
    of the keys. Now the church walls seem to shudder,

                the pipe mouths
    recoiling upon the seeming pantomime of his performance,
        a magic dumbshow of silently flicking the keys
    with velvet-soft fingertips. And there is no way I can fathom
            the hairlinefine exchanges
between his ten fingers' prowl of three keyboards and those distant
tall pipe-groanings,

pipe-wailings . . .
We'll embark, today, on our mother-son, off-the-beaten-path
            Island treks. So we attend
        to his genial warnings. The bars are all dangerous. But back
        in the ghettoes—*we call it Over the Hill*—the risk
of muggings, or worse, is critical. In broad day light. Chamber-
    of-Commerce
        won't hear of it, but, night or day, no hill or backwoods
            sector is safe! Then,
                            why has *he* stayed on
        these six months, braced for still another six, grit
            and pluck
    stamped on the cast of his jaw, his tall slender profile,
        orange-freckled face, neck and arm. Now he stands,
    for a moment, flashing his smile in the lit column of dust motes
            whirling in a pool of sun
that pours through the skylight. He signals the three black nuns
in the chapel doorway

to step back.
So doing, their twenty-odd local charges (boys and girls
            in equal numbers: ages
        five to nine, say) come racing to the organ bench. He resumes,
            playing his own transcriptions of nursery songs,
        Christmas carols, a few native Island hymns—the children singing
            out of tune,

getting the words wrong, no two in sync, but all
    finding another home
                to inhabit in the piped
    lullabies and jingles. Two forward children squat
        on the floor
near his feet, staying just clear of those pumping knees,
    intrigued by his undulations—the split second
reflexes of his feet floating over the pedals. A round-faced
        petite girl clambers
upon the organ cabinet, and sits, cross-legged, alongside
keyboards, memorizing

taps of his keys
beneath her legs. Two boys squeeze next to him, on opposite
        ends of the bench; while many
    form a ring around his seat, arms on each other's shoulders.
    He sings with them, not to lead the tunes, but more
to tag along. The churchwomen scowl, from time to time—threaten
        to send away
    the few least controlled kids, but he calms them all
        with his *Hush, now!* (finger
                to his lips). The children,
    asway, appear to dance from the hips, their legs bobbing
    in place . . . *I*
see two dozen blackbirds, or ravens, perched on his shoulders,
    his balding scalp, weightless, hopping on jointed-twig
legs across his redhaired curly forearms, alighting on his knees,
    his wrists. And one blackbird
lands on the tip of his nose, both perfectly still. Now it's
a black butterfly.

Those soft wings,
flapping, turn to petals of a black carnation, which falls
    to his shirt lapel . . . I waken

from a standup daydream, a bird romance, the blond organist
    still playing singalong tunes—the kids humming offkey,
while they follow their holy guides, public maidservants (in God)
    to the school
    van parked in the rear, their short midday recess
      come to a close . . . He fears
                        he's losing his touch
  at the organ knows he may well fail his instrumental
    M.A. exam
when he sails back home to Seattle it's been such a hot summer
    can't practise when he perspires so much for weeks
    he's been soaking in his own stale body fetors . . . No less
      absorbed in his Bach scores,
for carrying on two conversations with mother, with me—he blossoms
musical feast for us.

The Dungeon Amorist

(Fort Charlotte, Nassau, Bahamas)

We idle, circling the wide hilltop courtyard of Fort Charlotte,
                    and bypass the central
        square guardhouse—boxlike—which displays   *First visit*
                a few stuffed scarecrow
        model prisoners, immortally stooped & visible
                behind the window bars.
    The pebbly surface of our stroll is a roof to the Fort's
            labyrinth of underground passageways,
                    the stone hill's
                    interior carved by thousands
                        of slaves

chopping and hacking burrows in rock with the metal pickaxes:
            in three years of back-warping
        excavations, those chaingangs hollowed out
                a hideaway fort
        of the interior . . . We lift a central trapdoor,
                begin our slow descent
    into the buried fortress: the upper chambers, mess hall
            and living quarters; below, the dungeon
                    and torture
            compartments—long low crawl space,
                    the upright

    narrow cubicles scooped into the floor, each a small arsenal
                of ghastly penal hardware
            outlasting the victims and mutilators
                alike, for hundreds
    of years . . . The floors are lit by low portable lanterns,
                tucked in random corners.
    In each descending staircase, both walls are perforated
        by long grooves of varying widths—often,

blasts of air
seem to emit from these apertures
(wind vents,

or ducts?), as if air conditioning pumps had been installed
to cool modern visitors.
But our burly gruff "Bahamahost"
protests—his deep bass,
throaty bulletins delivered with afflatus of blurted
sermons: "Whoosh! Wind flies
through the fort, from hill summit to foot. Wholesome currents
circulate through air flues. No fans, no hidden
AC Units
whirring silently behind the walls—
it's all

natural ventilation . . . " He bids us reflect upon the genius
of architects who monitored
the mass dig: endless chains of pickax crews,
daily scoopouts of rock
shavings raised from below in canvas sacks, or leather
slings suspended by thick ropes
from pulleys, and carted away in wheelbarrows. They lacked
any supply of low-grade explosives
to shorten
the work time. Reduce the manpower
hours. *Years!*

But excavators of modern mines, despite nitro powder charges,
pile drivers and power drills,
have lost the ultrasonic Ears of those dig
architects—who could hear
deepearth rumbles, the quietest shifts along fault lines.
They sensed the minimal heave

and sway of shelves of quartz and shale miles under the cliff,
miles under the surrounding Carib Sea;
and they guessed
the stablest circuit of tunnels, guessed
the ideal

pattern of flues to conduct the maximum flow of trade winds
through the Fort corridors
and passages. The hums, tones, hisses
and echoes of breezes—
swirling through the magic wind tunnels above—are soughs
of gale winds magnified
in the upper channels. Gull screech and high-pitched wind wails
dissemble inhalation through a giant hurt lung's
bronchial tubes.
The hill of rock draws a breath of its own.
It whirls

around us, ruffling our blouses and shirt sleeves. Currents lick
our ankles. They crawl up
our pant legs, tickle our groins and armpits.
"Fresh air. Freshened breath.
It is all natural, brother. The natural trade winds cool
man-dug cave passages
of the Fort, natural currents endlessly circulating.
She is my dark Beauty. Oh listen
to her breathing!
She whistles me into her hollows,
lovely wind

channels, her lantern-lit low halls. Now she sweeps me along
on her sighs, wind-wails
of her breath, I, her twenty years inmate
and intimate. She

my gallows, my treasure! Fort Charlotte, my sweet—my secret
delight . . . " Is it all an act,
a grand Vaudeville charade? Or is he a man in High Love,
demon possessed, the perennial guide
and wanderer
through Fort Charlotte's recesses,
tunnels,

his daily haunts the aisles of her catacomb? . . . It's a ghoulish
love, a passion for corpses,
we hear chanted in his great barrel-chested
guffaws. *Cadaver love!*
And indeed, her lower chambers are vaults of a tomb: the fort
deeps, fort bottom levels,
are hived with cells of a Folk Mausoleum. The folk myths
of his robust oratory clamor
about the walls!
He bellows the ill fortunes
of hundreds

of limbs torn asunder on stretching blocks, tongues pulled out,
eyes stabbed with hot pokers:
the many subtle and varied ingenuities
of torture mimic—
grimly—acts of love in his lavish and prolonged lingering
over details of the horror.
He burbles and snorts a ghastly tableau: layers and layers
of incinerated bodies, great metal trunks
of heaped-up ash
dumped in the sea, at intervals—
all drowned

in gushed titters, baritone blasts of hurly-burly laughter.
And oh, how he loves to hear

the echoes of his own chortled vibrato
ricochet from passage
to passage (*ho-ho-ho*), redoubling through the many cells
of the honeycomb death house.
This two-hundred-pound bear in his sixties, gray sideburns,
silver-tinted black beard, for all his loquacious
spiel billowing
through the many tunnels of castle
underground

as prodigal as the endless bounty of trade winds that pour
through vent holes—he is tireless!
His huffing and puffing on stairways is surplus—
not loss—of breath,
breath undiminished for all his gargled Falstaffian
great Belly Laughs. The saga
of tortured spirits interred in the Fort's Memory Ear
is soothed, its pain lessened, himself a princely
host, gentle helpmate
to the flocks of visitors. He proffers
recipes

stylishly worded, for our comfort and safety: a verbal kin
to actual cane, brace, crutch,
medicine tablets—his instant and steadfast
hand under the elbow
of any Soul taking a stair too short, or too fast; shields
a forehead from batter by low-
hanging rock partition with his dear wide palm (no time
to howl "Duck!"); spots a trip in a floor crack
a full half step
before imperiled footfall; detects
half-formed

tears in an eye; listens for the half-uttered sobs in a throat
choked up; whiffs an onset
of fainting spell before the beleaguered
face pales and forehead
begins to droop—in time to dispense anodyne of schnapps
or smelling salts; and dispels
any heartsick pall in the spirit with his heady, roguish,
slapdash, lumbering jest . . . As, Mother,
he feeling—oh!—
a special endearment to *you,* he bows
to curtsy

your elf-slight diminutive carriage on each of a dozen-odd
overlong deep stairs, the steepest
ramp dropping through a rounded well in the rock,
last juncture from the Fort
dungeon arena's complex of cells to the hill foot exit,
a sort of bottom trapdoor.
He promenades you, his slim queenly guest of seventy-five,
failing to show *no* favoritism to a fellow
rare Sister
spirit. You trade movie mag and *National
Enquirer*

gossip column tales and squibs: the decline of past five U.S.
Presidents; the rising star
of Black Women in Bahamian politics
and world business;
the inside dope on bush-league Bahamian ball players
and middleweight boxers
who are sure bets for world champ futures; the canonization
and crowning of Aretha, the top Soul
or Gospel voice,
today, tomorrow, and beyond the future's
future . . .

Woman's Tongue

Our first daylight drive to Bridgetown . . . The stream
of traffic, congested
on the narrow
cobblestone roadway, is endless—
but few other cars. It's all foot traffic:
schoolchildren, uniformed, in clusters or smaller
fleets, rarely a single child
walking alone; housewives waddling to and from market,
deep baskets (empty
or full) balanced on their heads;
flocks of goats,
chickens and woolless sheep . . . After miles and miles
of tall cane rows, blocking most views of nearby scenery,

shock of blank farmlands, just planted with yams,
beans, vegetable seeds:
we see dozens
of small long-necked white birds,
scattered everywhere, hopping and poking
in the newly-turned soil: cattle egrets (you call them
cowbirds), they're ferreting for lumps,
rich nodules of predigested oats in the fresh manure.
They persevere,
snaring morsels from the dung
droppings, choice
tidbits speared with each peck, each scalpel incision
of those long tapered bills. "Will they deplete all soil

nutrients?" I ask. "What will fertilize the crops?"
"Ha! They rid young sprouts
of killer plant
aphids and pests, a *friend* to crops.
There's enough turds for all, and plenty
to spare." But the regal prancers, springing from dung

cakes to flattened pies, never tire,
never sate their appetites, nip and spear, stab and gorge
their slim bills.
"They should be as obese
as pelicans,"
I say. "How do they stay so slender?" But you brood
upon the avidities of *woman:* open wounds of your divorce—

haunted, still, by images of all love's rewards
and bonuses gone sour.
Grave emblem
sears, flickers before your eyes:
That woman's skull, years after death,
wagging its jawbone up and down, full sets of teeth
chattering yet. The silent jaw—
like an obsolete oil derrick still pumping the drained
well—is cursed
by a nervous tic that defies
rigor mortis.
It keeps jerking open and closed, from side to side,
for eternity, a carryover of the ceaseless nag, bicker,

nitpicking over every trifle, slip—that poisoned
the last years of a twenty
year wedlock.
I shudder! The looming mirage
you grimly lyricize flickers on our wind-
shield (shadows cast by frond tips of the tallest cane);
and worse, I seem to hear skull bones
yammering in the wind. "What is that ghostly crackle
overhead?" I yelp.
Your face a sinister grin, you brake
to a roadside halt,
stepping from the driver's seat and pointing upwards:
"Woman's Tongue! See how they flap and creak in the wind!

So many Woman Tongues in motion at once." I stretch
my neck through the car window,
while taking in—
at a glance—whole galaxies
of the flat tongueshaped dried pods, dangled
from the tops and all visible fringes of the long row
of trees bordering the road edge.
When the wind blows, they all shake and rattle in chorus.
I could mistake them
for a vast flock of black grackles
or warblers,
but for your verbal notation: "Hear them whisper
and hiss—like women *shushing*," you say. Your eyes roll,

as if they put you in a trance, and when the wind
grows stronger, the shush sounds—
oddly isolate
and distinct in light breezes—
become a single irreducible crackle,
which spreads and spreads in the distance around us . . .
And you say, "That's the way it was
when the whirlwind of marriage blew hardest, that army
of vile locusts
sizzling and roaring. Behind
any casual hurt
or misgiving, the din became impossible to escape,
the whole world of sound given over to the drawn-out

flapping of those unstoppable tongues." *Wind dies.*
Grating clatter upon our ears,
moments before,
lulls to a stammer, the few clicks
spaced out—at intervals—from one end
of the thick clump of trees to the other. *Soft rattlings.*

Those quiet aftershocks, residues
of pandemonium of vengeful tongue-clucks, tongue-sputters,
seem more noiseless
than silence itself. And in this sad
epilogue, knell
to our fierce chorale of furies, you recall tender
passing laments of early betrothal—pain quickly dulled,

the mournful voice but one quaver from gay teasing;
those easier griefs shaken
by a straw's tickle
under the chin, your wife's tongue
flirting with the bass notes of the dirge.
Her voice softened with kisses and laughter, she'd relent
to the gentle wind's caress,
as do these immature pods in late fall and winter, rinds
still moist and green.
But in the long hot season, their skins
grow thin and taut—
they dry out quickly! The pods wilt, a one-year cycle.
There's no turning back. The trees lose their leaves in May

and June, exposing the dried pods to roughest winds
in the season of storms—
toward the day
of the last worst gusts. *Midsummer.*
All the Woman Tongues fibrillate at once,
like heart muscles run amok—they wildly tremble and quake,
taking small comfort from matched
agonies of their fellow tongue flutterers, their comrades
in dry-voiced angers;
the dried-out pods, cracked and flaking,
fall to earth . . .
New whole forests of Woman's Tongue trees, it is said,
may spring from a single burst-pod's wind-wafted seedlings.

Queen of the Billiards

On the first eve of Carnival, night of the Queen
    contest, I dine on the hostel
        terrace overlooking Castries' Harbor.
            The hostess, much
                senior to the teenage waitresses,
            mid-twenties, say (svelte
        in lustrous black taffeta dress; short cape
with lace trim), takes elegant slow steps, escorting me
    to the premiere Harbor View
            two-seat table. Then she sidles
        out the back door, nods to the hidden bar hostess, drops off
            her high heels and—in one long stride—scoops
            a pair of slippers with upcurled toes. She shuffles

across a hardwood floor to join a tense parlor game
    in progress in the smoke-filled
        back room, she the absentee participant
            whose next shot
            is so nervously awaited—
        the expectant hush
    draws me to the rear exit. Unobserved,
    poised behind the decorative carved door jamb, I peer
        at a fast-moving game
            of billiards. Three agile men compete
        with the black-gowned hostess, her moves with a cue stick
            swift, exact, wholly free of excess.
            The electric snap of her delicate thin wrists,

her eel-like slender black arms, crisp pop of the cue
    and click of ball upon ball—
        all bespeak a style near flawless. Two men,
            distant friends
            to the proprietary couple
        (manager, chief hostess),

dressed in knockabout leisure suits,
tease and snicker, warmly, between her virtuoso
     shots. Her calls, delivered
          in sharp creole patois ("seeks bawl
     in de syd pahk't, Mon"), elicit fond jeers—so relaxed,
          they forgive her for winning. Their eyes
          applaud her talent. But the manager, in *Dreadlocks*

hairdo, three-piece suit and suspenders, who is
     courting her and hates to lose
          (failed wooer, too, I'd hazard), casts zigzag
               finger shadows
               across the aimed trajectory
          of her next slow shot.
          When the chicanery of finger
     puppets flops, her lucky streak unchecked, he performs
          hexy hand-hoops, fists and V's
               over the ball, circling the chalked tip
          of her cue stick in motion (waist-bent, he shakes the broad
               table with his reach), chanting voodoo
               curses and bugaboos . . . She frowns, but tolerates

his worst pranks. They are his *Reggae* prerogative.
     At last, she misses a routine
          flick shot. He snatches the cue from her, lines up
               his ricochet
               side-cushion poke with great flourish:
          Rastafarian who stalks
          prize game, he executes
     his combinations with princely attack, palms thumping
          the velvet table top—a drum beat . . .
               He whoops a cry of triumph, two classic Ace
               shots in a row! Then, murderous quiet bathes the gnat-thick

hall. Individual dust motes divebomb
the table like a storm of asteroids, meteorites . . .

Hand slips, in mid-shot. The long tapered rod squirms,
  jiggles in his grip, and the ball
    flies askew. Leaps the hurdle of side cushion. Cracks
      glass panelling
        in the antique double doors. "Scratch,"
      she murmurs, while he,
    in fury, swings the cue back and forth
  like a cracked whip, rips the felt cover from end to table
    end, exposing the unfinished
      wood—flesh pink—beneath the gash. "Foul play.
    You jumped!" he threatens her. Now both men restrain his arms,
      while—the cue stick smashed across his knee—
        he waves wood icicle spears, Zululike, with each hand . . .

Sunday: My Throat Afire

(Castries, St. Lucia)

Sunday. My throat
afire. All public pharmacies bolted
shut . . . A local child,
decked out in bright greens—the parish school
uniform—routes me down a wavery path through woods
to the country store. I lose
the pathway twice for tall weeds, spillover thickets,
fallen logs,
and nearly collide with a vine-crisscrossed
wall. *Another door,*
double-boarded over. I turn, thinking to reverse my steps, and pick

my way back
to the main road—but I halt. Overhead,
a voice offers help,
help for all troubles. A tread of sandaled feet—
upon the roof—pads near. "It's my throat," I'm saying.
My finger points to the faulty
organ: "It's nothing, a trifle. Cough drops, any flavor
or brand, will do,
please." But the voice slides over the edges
of my last few words,
neutering their drift: so much devalued currency, out-of-date coin,

cancelled checks.
Shaman or necromancer, voice oily
and unctuous, his tone
is an odd blend of stock-broker and bookie.
Shop closed on Sunday. He and a handyman on the roof
for repairs, or remodelling.
He signals his co-roofer to rest until his return, leaps
down the ladder

(dropping three or four steps at a lunge),
the while he counsels me
on the hidden "infestations, a pestilence" lurking behind common

throat ailments.
"We mustn't just numb de symptoms, y'know.
Gots to stifle de roots!"
He unbuttons his lightweight silk jacket, pokes
two fingers in each of six small vest pockets hand-sewn
in vertical rows: he searches,
distractedly, for a small parcel lost amidst the scramble
of tinkly metals—
keys, coin, nails, pocket clippers, medicine
vial?—with each flick
of his rummaging fingers, he tags and inventories a familiar

stockpile of dopes
and remedies. The smirk of known finds,
undoubted cure-alls, curls
the corners of his mouth as he retracts his hand
from the bottommost slim pocket, a square yellow packet
pinched between thumb and index finger.
The sealed paper sack is frayed, brown-stained at the corners.
"Liver salts,"
he enunciates, as one who chants
Medical Latin, and hands
me the pouch: "Very strong. Potent. In its most concentrated pure

form. Just a pinch
of this powder, mixed with water, kills
de pain. You must gargle,
at intervals . . . " He groans a sample of Afro-
Gargle, a passable—if wobbly—baritone aria. But first,
his treatment: a surgical tactic,

the prime guarded secret of his pharmacological clan (six
generations
of his family's practice of paramedics'
and drugstore expertise), drawn
from his private store of homecrafts—"herbal arts." He rattles off

polysyllabic
names! Instruments, natural medicines,
elixirs, herbs, potions—
he might be an Austrian Count, or Duke, who boasts
of matchless casks in his private wine cellar . . . We enter,
stooped, the low doorway of a thatched-palm
hut, iglooshaped, half-darkened. He seats me on a tall stool,
snapping the chain
under the one bare electric bulb, dangled
directly over my eyes,
blinding at first. Then he mutters, by turns, odd magic stigmata

of my disease
and arcane techniques of primitive
crypto-surgery he, alone,
in the Antilles Island Chain is wholly certified
to perform for their cure . . . I rise to my feet, opposed
by a firm hand pressing me floorward,
the low ceiling bonking my scalp. "The gargle will cure me,"
I feebly protest,
trying to shuffle past him to the door, he
a pillar, immovable guard . . .
He croons a song of my lethal symptoms, never glancing in my throat,

which he proclaims
is "torrid with rawness," "an inflammation,
or conflagration, of the glands
and tonsils." I'm waiting out his prattle, my eyes

now accustomed to the glare of the one bright bulb halfway
lighting the dim cluttered recesses
of the squalid infirmary hut: soiled sheets and bedclothes
in one corner,
cobweb tatters netting the neglected linens;
along one wall, a zigzag row
of assorted bottles, packages, surgical tools—and most striking,

I can just make out
a series of objects suspended by a wire
affixed to the ceiling.
Scanning from roof to floor, I note a hodgepodge
of amulets, charms, bones (rabbit's foot, monkey's paw,
whatnot?), a stained pair of decrepit
cracked old shoes at the bottom, an anchor, a few inches
above the floor—
the chain of talismans, or fetishes, shaken
by winds outside the hut,
the whole thatched dwelling asway, from time to time, in the midday

gusts . . . My attention
riveted to this display of obeah gewgaws
and gimcrackery, I ignore
my host's pacings from side to side, and his arming
himself—to my sudden alarm—with Q-tips and large cotton
swabs! In one hand, a bottle of amber
liniment; in the other, as he bends near, bidding me
to drop my head
back and "open wide," I see a scalpel's
part-hidden sharp edge flash
between two balls of cotton (wedged tight, so to conceal a weapon) . . .

His handyman
slinks behind him now, both guerillas wrapped

in soiled aprons—the semblance
of surgical gowns, complete with ill-fitting rubber
gloves and gauze face masks. The hunched assistant's figure
is blurred, his hands slyly concealed
behind his boss's shoulders. But he carries bulky implements,
so I surmise,
observing the long shadows of his hands
and their tall contents
cast on the hut wall, a bluish flame flickering from one! A bunsen

burner, or blowtorch?
The head Shaman steps forward, hands poised
to commence glum surgery . . .
I'm up from the stool, scamper out the low-roofed
portal at a single bound: "No hospital Emergency Room
stunts for me," I clown, my terror
no less urgent for the guise of farce. A rubberized claw
snatches, deftly,
the prescribed liver salts from my limp
hand. The masked gargoyle squeals—
in a voice at once testy and hysteric—"I'm finished with you . . . "

The Banana Madonna

En route to Roseau
Valley Church, we pass defunct
sugar mills, a few
kept up as *ruins*—followed by lush crops
of banana trees and coconut palms, both casting much shade
and cooling our passage through St. Lucia's
rolling pastures. (Banana images, profuse in local Church
Art, glut our talk) . . .
Never have I seen so many unpicked bananas at once—
this plantation the richest,
so near to harvest: the thousands of green firm tubes wrapped
in bundles, thousands
of green hands upon hands upon hands—
fingers woven together, wound
about the stalks and vines . . . It's the great *Siesta*
of banana trees. The proliferant orchards
doze, Pater and Mater Familias Banana sleeping the long repose
of blessed hands crossed in their laps, crossed
over ample bellies,
green fingers interlocked. *Sleep. The sleep*
of bananas

toward harvest, while the sun's slow yellow light seeps,
dilutes the vine-tough green of rinds. I dream
the slow quiet goldening of the crops . . .
We leave behind the last plantation, bear right
down an elegant short cobblestone side road: "Here, stop!"

The church's brick
face leaps in front of my hood—
before the road gives
any sign of quitting. Our engine idling,
we step from the car. My eye follows golden loops in the jigsaw

pattern of stained-glass panelling
in the tall windows raised above our windshield:
two bright haloes
highlight the upper panes, many panels of varied colors
fitted into a composite
design below. Your arms, shaping coils and parabolas in the air
over our heads,
guide my view from the halo above the mahogany
haired woman's forehead locks
to the marvelous flowing banana forms, arched like horseshoes,
boomerangs, erect phalluses—
but always, the banana is the norm all bold variations branch
away from, or return to. Likewise, the borders
and outer fragments
of stained-glass mosaic are all banana
twists. They begin

outside the portrait's visible outline, but undulate
deep into the midsection of the tableau.
Other banana twirls and prongs,
snaking around margins of the painting, appear
to flow into the banana orchards in neighbor plantations,

the lines of crops
we'd just passed in our Datsun repeated
in the crisscrossing color veins
of glass—banana shapes not merely copied,
but transplanted . . . Ivy, climbing the church's walls and sending
forked twin vines across nearby fields,
blends nature and wall no more seamlessly than stained-
glass banana designs
which intertwine the faces and necks of mother
and child suckling her breast.
Strings of half-peeled bananas swirl into the mother's neck-veins,

her breast-veins.
The child, perhaps, imbibes banana milk;
while mother and child, alike,
inhale banana-flavored air: "She is my Banana Madonna!"
you are saying. And yes, faces and busts
of baby, Madonna, seem a tapestry woven of banana vines, half-open
banana peels. Silhouettes of bulky unpeeled bananas,
winding around frames
of glass panels, overspill their outlines . . .
Banana curves

and loops flow into curlicues that become the mother's
ear lobe, her dimpled chin, long slanted neck,
the baby's puffed cheek: bananas the leaf,
stem, root; Madonna and child the blossom—ripe fruit
of stained glass to be plucked by the Congregation's Eye.

The Mural of Wakeful Sleep

For Dunstan and Derek

Quattrocento put in paint
On backgrounds for a God or Saint
Gardens where a soul's at ease;
Where everything that meets the eye,
Flowers and grass and cloudless sky,
Resemble forms that are or seem
When sleepers wake and yet still dream . . .
—W. B. Yeats

I

Despite the darkened
pews and cloisters, I see—at once—
Roseau Church is deep,
spacious. You hasten to the interior
(having seated me in a rear pew bench), throwing open each set
of barred shutters in succession . . . Great columns
of daylight come hurtling into the hall with the force
of physical bodies—
hurled masses of light, fierce locomotives of fire—
pouring through the window
gaps. You advance to the front chapel, taking long strides. My stare
overleaps
your imperially tall, slim frame and connects
with the immense altar mural
behind the low stage. The mural ascends to the chapel
roof, fills the entire front wall,
the stage pedestal as wide as the whole church . . . The human figures
so lifelike and proportioned, a parishioner
must forget the mountainous
breadth of the bodies, the faces luminous
with a light

that baffles the eye. *How can mere pigment, slapped
on a brick wall, simulate the color of flesh*

vivid with passion of work's holy
instant—or love's, play's, music's? Size eludes
beholders of the whole wall at once. Eyesight flits

from corner to corner,
from midpoint to outermost borders
(which neither terminate
nor frame the scenes, so much as flow
outwards into the life bristling on the far side of Church walls) . . .
As moviegoers forget the sheer giantism
of human images flickering upon technicolor screens,
stunned, say, by puny
usher chasing a child across the theatre stage, both
fleshly smaller-than-life
townsfolk tiny enough to be hidden in the pants-cuff of silver screen
newspaper Mogul;
or in the pencil case of his Ace heroine
reporter—so I, today,
gasp at the optical incongruity of your six-foot-six
gangling figure, insectlike, poised
on tiptoe in front of the mural, a praying mantis silhouette (I can't
make out your features in the dim
stage-shadowy glimmers,
only your long slim skeletal outline),
italicized,

highlighted on the brilliant colors of mural backdrop.
But no, the painted wall is all foreground, scenes
and players lit from within by the gouache
gum shine of your passion; though your own body,
waving and pointing to *this* musical performer, to *that* steel-

helmeted construction
crewman perched in his cab cage

and leaning forward
to shift the long-handled controls,
is *incorporeal* in this light. Your noble physique pales. *A film
of cobweb? A wisp of gauze netting?*
*Diaphanous, in the outstretched stance of a lean electric
short-trim-bearded
hauntingly lovely black man, wafted across the altar
pedestal as if blown,
gently, by trade winds passing through the wide unshuttered windows
cross-ventilating
the Great Hall.* You are shouting the names
of sainted and common folk,
alike, blurting short pithy captions under each figure,
sharing anecdotal secrets from your life
that fed the townspeople of your dream fresco—tales of your family
and domestic setting, rumor or gossip
reported of neighbor
village tilted for disguise, yet mirrored
in dream

pictures they nourished. Now you bend forward at the waist,
and I must stand up tall on my low pew bench to follow
your graceful hand tracings of action scenes
in the mural's bottom quadrants. Half-stooped, you wave
your pipe cleaner arms, prancing to and fro. Wide sideways dashes

of antelope or gazelle!
But your matchstick-doll-torso (*Man
the Creator who unwound
the whole Glory Cosmos of wall mural
from the spool of his earth dweller's fantasy*) is narrower of girth
than the Christ Child's rattle, shorter
than the baby's little finger curled around its handle;
your whole grizzled head

smaller than the O of Mary's fondly cooing pursed lips . . .
And I know a moment
of terror! You may be swallowed up by a mouth of your own creation,
or lifted
and crushed by infant fingers. You grow
dimmer in the fading light.
Your skin ashen, your faded denim suit looks ghostly,
illusive, almost *gaseous,* as compared
to the opaque whole colors of your life studies—township of mortals
and divinities mingled in a chromatic
pastel blend of kin:
a family of folk Beings and Saints
ashimmer

in the story Saga of the wall. Our own flesh—yours *or mine*—
seems phantasmal, we the copies, the painting Souls
the originals: you the puppeteer's
marionette whirled by the invisible guide wires
of your actors, your models . . . And now, seated beside me, you

marvel at your happy
Fate. That avalanche of energy. Providential
gush. The creative furor
which swept you through the absurd commission—
a seven-day time limit!—to complete Roseau Church's altar mural
for a token fee, three hundred West Indian
dollars. Hardly enough money to pay for the paint.
(" . . . *then, you can pass*
the hat." "Yes," I replied. Nothing looks impossible to me.
Just imagine the jams
I get into.) You tucked a pallet bed in the vestry corner, a hot plate
to boil water,
then began blocking out some eight hundred
square feet of church wall

for the vast bucolic, choosing the countryside and outdoors
format—though you worked by candle light
through the whole week, doors and windows bolted shut every minute.
Now I picture you mixing the colors, working
at all hours to bring back
with paint and brush the light of day
you shut out

with heavy wooden shutters. No clocks. And no sun to tell you
it was time to rest, short naps snatched, seated upright
against the back wall (near the pew we shared,
today); you dozed off, briefly, eyes half open, perhaps,
while you studied the design in progress on the wall opposite . . .

II

Never sleeping by plan,
or by scheduled intent, it seemed as if
the painting continued
in your sleep. So often you would *come to,*
with a start, amazed to find the bongo drummer's two tandem drums
placed under his hands' blurred thumps
before you remembered fixing the planes for drum tops,
drum bottoms, beneath
the birdlike flutter and flap of the performer's palms—
while you slept, standing,
one arm braced to hold your knobby starved-thin skeleton parallel
to the wall.
What force impelled your arm, wielding
the many-colored brush?
What genius for a local face coursed through your sketch
marks—the few blobs of color? A flash
of Being, a fleeting glimpse of joy or pain, crossed each profile.
The human moment trapped by your brush's

swift magic . . . The hours,
days, minutes disappeared, swallowed
by moves

of the brush, you balancing on higher and higher ladders,
and finally makeshift scaffolds, patched together
from old picture frames, discarded rope,
wire, and other debris. To daub color, to mark strokes
was all. Food and sleep fell away. *To paint is to draw breath—*

never before your joy
in art so total, as if the paint itself
issued from your bones.
Its source had seemed the many small bones
in your wrists, your ankles, and the ladder-rung-bruised metatarsals
of your pained foot arches. Smallest bones,
in your somnambulist fantasy, liquefied—one by one—
to yield more paint,
more paint, turning to sainted flesh (you'd recalled
poring over the skeletons
pictured in Medical Anatomies, a boy held spellbound for unnumbered
hours by magic
intertwinings of the many, many tiny bones
in the articulations of ankle,
wrist, foot instep . . .) In your slow martyrdom of self-
dismemberment, first you proffered wrist bones:
perfectly lubricated small bulbs, metacarpal by sliding metacarpal,
melted down to illuminate and golden
the paint . . . This moment,
seated by my side, you speak of your slow
starvation,

and I seem to behold the small bones of your bare ankles,
bare wrists, shining with inner light. *They glow*

again. They are lit embers. Gold coals.
They ache with the twin tasks of lifting the brush
from pail to wall, pail to wall; and lifting your weary hips

from rung to ladder rung,
a rank pain that throbbed and deepened,
in time, as nails pounded—
slowly—into hands, into ankles, must deepen
(though neither of us speaks of Christ, neither mutters the words,
"crucify, crucify thin bones into paint,"
we both trace images of the Cross disguised—here
and there and everywhere—
in the mural's portraiture) ... Toward week's end,
so many times a day,
the pounding at the church door began: your wife, daughters, sons,
each howling
to you to come fetch the tray of food
they'd left for you;
complaints growing louder, if you hadn't touched
the last meal. But you opened the door
for no Soul—not wife or child. Food disappeared, from time to time,
but they must not stay, none be present.
You could be dying,
or mortally hurt from a fall, perhaps,
death plunge

from the odd towers of rudely assembled ladders, scaffolds.
They could see segments, wobbly and tilted off-center,
through peepholes in the closed shutters.
But if ever they stopped their strident voices for long
enough to listen, they heard you singing. Ah, you sang and sang

as you worked, finding tunes
and lyrics to match the elation you felt,

pouring your happy melodies
into the broad expanse of wall. For each idea
your hand daubed, others tumbled forth, redoubled. Your brushes
sped up. They raced the welter of images
taking fire in your eye, no way for hand or paint
to stem the unslowable
tide of mental pictures, rushing too fast, too fast,
shaking you on the ladder:
those vibrations set up, your bone bag swung one way, ladder assembly
the other.
Amazing to hear of it, this rabid ladder dance
of a new art scale come
to birth! How lucky the wall itself didn't collapse,
some vibration cycles known to shatter
glass, crystal, forged iron . . . But you never lost your footing.
And the ladders absorbed your wildest
oscillations and bends,
while you sang of the Soul we imbibe
through paint.

Oh, we can lip paint soul, tongue paint, throat paint, sex paint . . .
Brain-sing paint soul! Finger and toe, palm and heel—all
touch zones blaze, aquiver with new paint life.
You kept your balance, and often, it seemed, the wall swayed
in time with the swathes of your brush, shifting its angle to catch

a revolving elbow's thrust
when you slipped; or softened to a cushion
for your lolled forehead
when you dozed, by fits and starts, still erect
on your ladder tops. Words of your song you forget, but your theme—
which roared in your blood and drummed
in your temples—found its dual outlets in your throat's
improvised melodies

and the mural's painted figures. You recite for me, now,
amidst scattered verbal
marginalia on the tableau's well springs: "Oh, people are running away
from painting.
I must, somehow, bring back *the world trend*
of painting." And last, your passion
to teach paint joy to children: "It must be Islandwide!
I won't have programs for elite schools, only.
I'll train art teachers, myself. No one else can motivate as I can.
The trick is, we can outwit death with colors!
Just give the children paint
and palette, twelve bright solid whole colors.
Then, step

back!" Your only pedagogic command: "Be free with color . . . "
You resume the running fact sheet of glosses, oral
footnotes, on the mural's life sources. *Joseph,*
Mary, and the Christ Child are Black, you an apostle
of Black Theology—profiled in leading West Indies Journals.

III

Joseph's regal forehead,
his high wide cheek bones and jaguarlike
forward pitch of the shoulders,
were modelled after an American basketball player
featured on the cover of *Ebony* magazine—his gaunt carriage risen
to the topmost limit of his highjump
while he executed a flawless *dunk* shot. His head was poised
just under the cover photo
metal net-hoop, transfigured, here, to a gold stark halo
levitated over his creased brow, his bare
upper body now darkly garbed. He becomes the mural's caped Guardian
Angel! His arms,

upraised, encircle holy mother and child—
a caretaker's pose;
while his glittering eyes project beams of light
across outlands of populous muralscape,
a human lighthouse or watchtower. The many folds of his voluminous
cape and undergown billow, as if windswept.
On either flank, his expanded
velours, a furrowing of the robe draperies,
suggest wings

hinted beneath the fabric, seraphic wing plumes braced
for imminent flight, his shoulder muscles rippled,
neck veins inflated with happy passion.
But the Madonna, curled in a round-shouldered
slouch, the baby suckling her breast, exhales icy serenity:

her face, waxen and impassive,
but lovely in its mythic proportions—
marbled purity of feature—
was fashioned from a West African mask
of the Earth Mother you'd copied from a museum rental collection
of anonymous works, a travelling art show
hired by several Windward Island nations, in succession,
funds raised by joint
campaigns of science foundations and art councils. The art
and science museum curators,
after heated debate, took turns with the exhibits—works of genius
and nobility
displayed with amazingly diverse captions
while rotated from one museum
to the other. But you, laughingly, report: "Not one *expert,*
amongst those art critics of either faction,
who haggled, month after month, for custody of the leased treasures—
not one, I say, who claimed to know the totemic

cast of features in each mask
as well as their very own son's or daughter's
telltale

face contours, recognized the true source of my Madonna;
so startled were they—one and all—by joy I breathed
into Black Joseph, Black Mary; by my rage
to rescue our Faith from its theology of death
and morbidity, to translate the Holy Beings into my Vision

of happy, happy earthiness!"
You smile, ardent to recount for me the random
finds that served as models
to your high fellowship of citizens and immortals.
Often, surprises in divulging your sources seem to brighten your eyes.
"Look again," you say, pointing to the central
tableau: "Man, woman and child are woven in a semiabstract
tapestry of capsules,
lines of face bones and shoulder muscles of the three figures
laced with geometric
ornamentation. But despite the detailed overlay of linework, filigree
of caricature,
these Holy Ones partake of the blooded life
of nature and the common man
spinning around them in the dozens of portraits and scenes
in peripheral sectors of wall." And I agree.
They both nourish, and take fire from, action scenes encircling them.
Columnar lines and parallel bars—generated
by the cubist perspective
of the oval centerpiece—pass outward, ribboning,
but they fade

into that naturalistic gallery of townsfolk. At bottom
center, guiding my eye slowly clockwise, you chortle

loud burly affection for the helmeted men
driving derricks, cat tractors, bulldozers: all chug-a-lug
beer-guzzling pals of yesteryear (at age fifty, two years back,

you'd vowed to renounce booze—
too much work slowdown). The reggae dancers
in one corner, bongo drummers
and calypsonian duet in the other, I follow
the eerily visible wave rumble lines of the drummers upwards. We settle
on masked dancers of a troop in carnival
costumes, one harlequin clown midway in a backwards
somersault, his oval pants-seat
marking a perfect bull's eye through the hoop formed
by his mates' four curved arms
joined at the wrists, suspended above his upwards-floating boot heels.
A musician
is rattling the percussive chac-chac beans
shaken in a long metal tube.
Both arms vigorously wield the instrument, while he,
too, appears to dance in high leaps,
one bent knee upraised against his chest, his lips wide with howls
directed, perhaps, at the boy in the uppermost
right corner, bare-chested,
who blows the horn of his queen conch shell.
A dour song

to the harbor dawn? Or bitter dirge to his sunken heart, love
stolen, his moans safely muffled from the public ear,
and the all-night masquerade? His solitude
not quite perfect, the song to himself carries to a seated
fisherman behind him, slumped in fog (but *we* can pierce that veil

of mist), hand cupping his ear:
who strains to listen for mourned laments

of the conch, nearly motionless
in his square sailed hand-carved cottonwood
dugout. So still is his boat upon the unrippled sheen of the bay,
so slack the one sleeping canvas drooped
from his slim mast, so well shall he keep the distraught
lover's conch-blown secret.
The lone shore birds cheep and scribble their thin-toed
cuneiform scrawl on the sand . . .
The softer music of the conch caps the mural's roof-high gold border,
which mutes
the raucous jabber of the calypso singers
and the chac-chac's unstoppable
sputter. By like diminishment, the blurred contortions
of the dance troop are becalmed by the woman
seated overhead, bent forward on her knees, hands pressed together,
fingerends pointed upwards in prayer, asway
from side to side, face lifted
toward a sunrise at sea. *Her least motions*
a sedate dance,

her dress is all of the sun. She amply fills the upper left mural
corner, wide gold head kerchief bulky—but evenly balanced—
over her gold-on-gold embossed lacework dress.
Gold necklaces and bracelets. Gold earrings. Her jewels displayed
in secret sun worship, this priestess of daybreak is the mural's fulcrum!

FROM

The Creole
Mephistopheles

1989

Girard, Girard

Why, we puzzle,
   does Viola choose,
      ever, near-midget or dwarfish
manservants,
   her hostesses
      all towering giraffes
      or great tubby
ostriches—the latter embellished
with lardy buxom charms. But none of the women,
      however nubile
         or maidenly, challenge Viola's
      midfifties'

      glamours. The hostel
         is run by that bevy
         of tall audacious demoiselles
who manage all
   check-outs, check-ins,
      the ledger, account books;
      hear complaints,
survey dysfunctions in plumbing, wire
circuitry, electric light fixtures, fans' bent blades.
         Three night porters
         (handymen, by day) fetch spare parts,
      tools; transfer

      bulky equipment;
         see to all repairs.
         Tiny and swift and agile, heights
under five feet,
   the men scurry about
      skittishly—their shoulders
      twisted one way,
hips pivoting the other. And we can see

they'd *have* to be built close to the floor to cover
     so much ground space
       per second per second. Night foreman
and day chief,

     near lookalikes,
       blend into the one
       tireless caretaker, who pops up
everywhere, face
    first, feet a blur;
      he's still running in place
      (like a swimmer
treading water), legs oddly stationary,
thighs pumping, when he greets my plea: *At your service,*
    Monsieur. Shortorder
      cook, for breakfast, lunch, poolside
or bedtime snacks.

    Ace lifeguard
      at the ready for pool
      rescues. Paramedic deputy braced
to administer
    emergency first aid,
      or pulmonary resuscitation
      from cardiac
arrest. Allhours' night clerk, who beds down
on floor and sleeps with one eye open. Steadfast guard,
      behind locked gates,
      who springs to full service at our wee
    hours knuckle rap.

    Surrogate uncle
      to small children, parole
      officer to miscreant sons of guests,

or to Viola's
   derelict offspring,
      alike. Services carried off
      as numberless
as hours per week of their vigilant fury
of labor—the men all the same body type, small-boned,
      squat, hyper-alert . . .
      But their fey supervisor, in a class
   apart, sports skin

      pigment two shades
         lighter; his bristly
         thick eyebrows and bushy mustachios
curled at far ends,
      earhair tufts untrimmed:
         all hairy puffs and twists
         seem to flicker
with his inner wraith, a sprite of soft wit
and quiet laughter—those waxed and crimped hair points
         of his fur express
         elfin cheer, broad smile aglimmer
   in brown eyes, always,

      but it rarely erupts
         from his winsome lips,
         unparted. A shy man sworn to tasks
of deed or ready word,
      his one word, *heedful,*
         is charged with the drift and scope
         of our palavered
fifty . . . Though Viola, his headmistress, claims
his allhours duty, the bondage of an indentured slave,
         it's those children

of all faiths, color, age, sex, who
manifestly *own* him.

The other six men,
    jockey-slim stewards
    reduced by bullying, perhaps, to bland
faceless *yesms, yessirs,*
    or the French equivalent
    (her ghostly eminence presiding),
    are mere makeweights,
factotums. But Girard, his banter to children
swirling through halls, down corridors, makes fond jest
    of infants' tears—
    his whimsy a resourceful high art
    for turning menial

    chores to play.
    By the very bounce
    of his worn sneakers, the pixieish
dance step of his turns,
    while racing around corners
    freighted with pagoda towers of trays
    in one hand, tall
columns of washcloths and towels balanced
on the other (never an eggshell cracked nor full teacup
    spilled), the very air
    breathed is charged with laughing gas,
    and we fall in fits

    of uncontrolled mirth.
    The children are beguiled,
    above all, by his perfect mimicry
of a dozen *barnyard*
    critters: goat, sheep, peafowl . . .

Best are his hearty dovecalls, owlhoots,
   finger-in-tongue
surprise parrot chirps; the enchanted kids' wails
charmed to sighs and titters: GIRARD, GIRARD, they chant,
      singly, or in chorus,
      leaving us struck with the name's innate
   wry twang, years after . . .

The Skateboard Throne: An Ode
to Citizen Amputees

(Jacmel, Haiti, Christmas 1983)

Warned to avoid
any fruit without peel or rind,
if we wish to prevent four-day-sieges of *peste,*
the stomach parasite
which befouls most local tap water
(we drink, strictly, soda
or brandname bottled water, French
seltzers—no Perrier sold in Jacmel go-carts), I glide
from mid market to far borders, laden
with three bananas,
four oranges and one large mango—this cargo
earmarked for our ambulatory lunch.
We've no time
to while away
hung up in local snack shops,
so much ground to cover before the Twilight
Express bus returns
to our lodgings in Port-au-Prince.
No *night* vans for us,
par Dieu!... We meander outwards
from the great-oval's center, feeling as if we wade
through layers of a colossal fruit
ball of humans,
each tier hotter than the last. We approach
the unroofed environs, leaving behind
all choice fruits—

pomegranates,
figs, mangos—in the market's
heart, commoner foods near the outer margins
in portable stands
dispersed through several orbits

beyond Iron Market's
      true perimeters. Here, we meet—singly,
    face to face—the cripples and deformed paupers, who,
   moments before, to my blurred city-
    blocks-distant sight,
      were mangled underfoot, while colliding
with the tumultuous hordes; though,
  now and again,
         low figures,
   wraithlike, dissolved their amputee
    bodies to fog balls, thin columns of mist.
    I beheld, squinting,
    through waves of glare and mirage
shimmer, that miracle!
    Who can explain how it is they scarved
   the smoke rings of their collapsing bone bags around
whole armies of upright shoppers
   who, mercilessly,
     galloped and marched upon them, their supine
or prostrate torsos devising instant
      gene mutations.

    Gaseous, swirly
they'd become, like windblown soots
   arisen from factory pipes, or house chimney.
    Their stunted bodies,
    shrunk-limbed or humped, though helpless
to dodge that infantry
    of market hustlers, were always saved—
   rescued, the last instant, by some divinatory marvel
of flesh dissolution. Their heads,
   necks and shoulders—
    grown incorporeal—flowed, unobstructedly,
through hips and thighs of the mob . . .

But now, up close,
                              each frail lout,
       lame pauper, appears to be insulated,
          set apart. An aureole of space, however small—
             luminous, inviolate—
          surrounds each bowed figure, kept intact
by the milling crowd,
                as if a thin layer of noxious poison gas
             envelops each legless upper torso revolving, slowly
and adroitly, upon his low throne
       of squarish skateboard.
                Breaststroking hither and yon on roller wheels,
       these are true swimmers of the bilgewater
                scummy riverine

             streets, where backwash
       of slimy pools stalled in roadway adorns
          the urban swamp. And one-legged beggar, atilt,
             crutchless, stays afloat,
          hobbling a jig on good knee and padded
stump (for histrionic
          effect on passersby?): this dance halts
          unfeeling aloof folks—dead in their tracks. I shrink,
       turning away from a burn victim,
          left half-face furrowed,
             her skin flaps curled in surgical disarray:
a false ear shape stitched in mid cheek
   mocks the ear lost;
                              her other half-face
       comely, unscarred. In full retreat, I brush
          shoulders with one whose face, strawberry-inflamed,
             is a pocked and pitted
          raw wound: noseless, reptilian, gaunt,
   eyes and mouth sunken,

near-lost in that ravaged facial topography;
   though his eyes blaze from lidless pits when he glares
and his mouth flashes a four-toothed-snarl
      when his lips stretch wide
         in a clown-quarter-moon downcurve frown, piqued
at a pinchpenny tourist: deformity
         less a handicap

      than a proud flag
waved: wares to be sold and resold, hawked
   in street fair auction, to high and low bidders
      alike . . . No piker passes
but operatic curse be howled, or hissed,
at the foreign tightwad;
         glob of well-aimed sputum shall catch him
behind the ear; or pellet gumball-tobacco-plug, fired
by basic slingshot, pang back of neck
   and capsize beret.
         (Now, huddled in streetcorner nook, unespied,
I celebrate the diverse mild tactics
   of pauper reprisals
               spewn at closefisted
transients) . . . All *my* piddling small change,
      from gift purchase, you divvied up—in equal shares—
         to the first handful
      of an endless siege of market hustlers,
your gifts always bestowed
      with jollity and gamy hand twirls. Your song
   of sparse handouts garnished with pleas for forgiveness,
   your trilled grace notes of apology
      outbeg the beggars
         to accept *our* thanks for not refusing paltry
   sums, the meagre alms. In spirit, evermore,
         you extend our feeble

driblets of charity.
Much ado, fuss, coaxing of the stingy
beside-her papa, taking their *side against* him,
he some manner of coin
purse hoarder, a locomotory United States–
personed Fort Knox. He balks,
she pleads: a father-daughter fencing bout.
His parry. Her thrust. His feints. Papa-lass tug-of-war
to feed and clothe the whole Third World
from their own poor nest
egg: she so close an ally to the starvers
and shirtless multitudes, all wiles
of verbal flourish
          in their own Creole
tongue and dialect, swiftly mastered
for repartee and barter: her bargain struck,
even with those who come
after the lucky few who've pocketed
her snippets of pence.
    He, too, half-welcomed as hip insider,
if lacking local sweet talk or facility with native
idiom, while she improvises verbal
insider's parley:
she their trusted spy in the enemy's ranks,
their helpmate and sponsor supreme,
    ever unstinting,

    her gaiety coffers
never emptied . . . Pallid children dance circles
around the Maypoles of our overnourished skeletons.
Unconcealed pouchy cheeks.
Paunch bellies. Ample butts. Rotundities,
all! Now I race ahead, you,
    penniless waif yourself, pawed and tugged

by relay teams of cuddler infants, a few tots so small
they may have gone on all fours last week:
    dwarf bipeds, wobbly
        and knock-kneed, they pierce your defenses;
your volley of appeals to me thinned,
    in distance, while youths
                        of all sizes and ages
    converge upon your stalled backpack loungy
        pale figure. And I'm shaken, for fear you be mugged—
            so many frazzled skulls
        barricading you, at once, I lose sight of you,
    but your gay palaver, ever
            audible, prevails over need *and* numbers. At last,
        you sweep toward me, trailing behind you—as if by pet's
    leash—your catch, his curled hand fastened, viselike,
            to your elbow: *each the prize*
            of each, I see, at your nearer approach; behind,
        the wan tousled heads alit with wonder
                    at your trick escape

            clamped to the forearm
        of a seven-year-old waif, dressed in scraps
            not fit for rags . . . You splutter news of Christophe's
                oral contract, a bargain
            just struck between you—he to serve an hour
    as your photographer's
            model; and he's to be paid four francs, plus
        one orange, one banana—up front: the latter, half-peeled,
    he ravenously *inhales,* thereby sealing terms
        of your verbal agreement.
            Ah! I wink my say-so, my fiscal O.K.,
drawing on my secret store of coat
    lining revenues . . .
                    How well your eye,

steady on, targeted the one surpassing model
    from throngs: in Christophe's soft face, quiet dignity,
        pathos and stoic calm
    mix; left eye blackened, jawbone swollen purply,
but his off-center slanted
        features are less disfigurement of floggings
    (family whip-or-fist blows to spur wage hustle fervor)
than sidewise tilt in gaunt facebones halfway
    between a true dark smile
        and smirk. You command his faithful moves for no fee
    but gay bravos, when you catch prize snapshot—
            your eyes' ardor

        and sparkle. *Your praise.*
He reveres your every whim and caprice,
    perfect marionette to the invisible strings
        drawn by your fingertip
    wands—pointing directions, while you mould
his pastel limbs, torso,
        neck into pivots, back bends, stoops
    and splits: all held in prolonged poses a pipecleaner doll
    could just manage—you the lost sister
    or favorite Great Aunt
        he's always pined to recover. So total,
those moves! His proud spare frame aches
    to please you, to win
                your nods, your happy
    sighs. These, these be rewards. In his glad eyes,
        a plenitude . . . His face scars, his flesh bruises
            notwithstanding, deprival
        speaks to me most in the diagonal twist
of the bent long clasp pin,
            rust-coated, that fastens the tattered
        wings of his faded lavender shirt lapels together.

That one hook-and-eye *safety* clamp,
   in place of a lost
      whole row of buttons, crosses his breastbone.
Just below, a thin strand of fishline,
     oft-tied and re-tied,

       simulates a belt
for his skimpy sackcloth shorts: looped
   through eye slit of the shirt pin above, it would keep
     those baggy adult pants,
   full-waisted, bleached-grey, from drooping,
floppily, around his ankles.
    One fragile pin, sole fastener and hookup
     for his bedraggled two-piece costume: both flanks of his shirt
tug at clip ends when he lifts his arms or twists
   his shoulders, to comply
     with rapid-fire guidelines for your photo poses—
exposing a wide ribbon of bare chest
in the gap . . . *And oh,*
         if the pin clasp bursts,
he'll stand naked! Or worse, his washboard
   corrugations of frail rib cage may pop open, as if clamp
    and fishline, alike,
  are unhealed sutures of a long wound, incision
running from his collar bone
    to his navel (no scar seal yet formed) . . . Now we stroll
   down unmarked dirt paths toward shore, while Christophe,
our shadow, tagalong, mimics our digressive
   slow pace. We dawdle . . .
    He looks away, then back over his shoulder—*he's*
forgotten us. And we, too, pretend to ignore
     your bewitched godson.

The Creole Mephistopheles

(Jacmel, Haiti)

I

Still a full hour before dusk,
   but there's no time to lose if we're to get
   a headstart back to Port-au-Prince before nightfall.
   We retrace our morning route—no detour or shortcut seems worth
      the risk of getting lost. Our van steward,
      gone sweet on you, offered to meet us on the hour at five; but we've
   taxied back a half hour
before the assignation, dropped at the outdoors
   vast bus depot. All twenty vans
      appear chock-full,
      each a last scheduled TAP TAP for the day
      heading north to the Capital. A few drivers, bumptious
   and aggressive, hawk for last passengers to fill their day's quotas,
      hustling chance passersby on the avenue,
   who may or may not be travelling today—but *we are,* and it shows
in our scrunched foreheads.
How can it be, that I mobilize no resistance
to the most churlish hawk's

      pounce—who confronts
   us at our cab door? We're to be his royalty,
chosen elite, hand-picked Crown Prince
   and Princess of guests, riding in the foam-cushioned
      front throne seat of honor, seatbelted, safely installed
         beside Monsieur
         pilot himself. He'll defer to our whims
   sooner than the whole cabin's, swears many a snorted vile oath
      to purely submit

to our bondage: *hollow, hollow.*
  But I crudely fall in with his prostration
  before us, his wheedling and vows queerly seductive
  in their horror . . . Deborah, pulling me close by net-shirt collar,
    mumbles in a low voice, "Dad, you've broken
  our promise to wait for André, who comes back for us in a half hour." ☉
"But André may forget,
or be detained," I reply. Exhausted and numbed
  by the day's havoc of our senses,
    I dread the onset
    of Haitian night, far removed from our Villa—
    so I choose an early start, smothering your demurs
  with papa-protector logic, though I hide my pangs of a betrayer heart.
    Soon we must make way for rotund Jean-Paul,
    wielding his bloated carriage, ponderously, down the narrow aisle
of his crowded bus,
as if the posterior thickset hunk of him heaves
  bulky melon pot forward

    in a wheelbarrow,
    a burly clownish walk that recalls scenes
in late Fernandel cinema farce,
  but lacking the classic comedian's hammy passion
    or gaiety. We know we're hustled, but we'll complete
    his roll, all the same:
      his quotas full, we can surely depart
for Port-au-Prince Capital City, forthwith. Though still at odds
    with each other,

    we're swept down a flood-ravaged
      side street, its furrows so deep and jagged
      the chassis bucks and wobbles like a child's toy wagon
    dragged across sewer grates (haste rules, no time to come to terms—
      our moral struggle quashed by survival panic);

now we're thrown into a mad grasping for strap, handle, floor frame,
O any fixed vertical
or diagonal rod, even upholstery springs fastened
down with rivets or steel bolts—
this become a world
in which our frail bodies have been altered,
suddenly, to loose seeds in a pod. The vehicle's least
bounce and lurch reveals all four shock absorbers have been ground
to pulpy steel wool . . . *Our first ride in a public*
TAP TAP! We'd been enticed, often, during our weeks in town, to take
short jaunts in Port-au-Prince
municipal TAP TAP, hardly as crammed with inmates
or as tattered and dilapidated

as this cross-country
variant of the bus prototype; rosy piquant
and picturesque exterior drew us
within (moreso, it seemed, than the huckster van pilot's
bribery and cajolements), disarmed of all caution, perhaps,
by the alluring hues,
starkly painted wood slats and iron frames:
bold whole colors—scarlets, greens, maroons, luminescent chartreuse,
rough equivalent

to the flamboyant color palette
of many Haitian painters whose works we admire.
DuFaut had lambasted our senses with his sharp-angled
hillscapes, hundreds of insect-tiny people zigzagging up and down
narrow thread roads and pathways; and despite shrunk,
minuscule scale, many distinct cameo portraits had arrested our eyes,
an unforgettable blaze
of primary colors in the patchwork of scanty clothes
and bare skin, mixed bushels of exposed
fruits and veggies, fresh-

picked, balanced on hikers' heads carting wares
to home or market; while oblique lines evoked the slant
of hillslopes, barren of foliage, where all trees had been shaved off
like so much worthless sagebrush, for sale to paper
and construction factories, or fires and fuel, topsoils washed away,
leaving most farmhills
no longer fit for *any* crops, planting or harvest.
And now, those starkly inked colors

adorning the bus walls
glimmered—to our eyes—like a happy extension
of the life of peasants and rural
families we passed on the country roads of our voyage
South, as if we'd been invited to partake of that life's
rude basic amalgam.
So we stepped inside, but knew, at once,
we were the more outsiders withindoors, more ostracized in spirit
for playing a partner

to dearths, to excruciated hardships,
not shared in body. And perhaps, we were swayed
by the worshiplike curve of those giant pink eyebrows
painted over the bus's windshields: the windows, then, mirrored light
like prayerful eyes bidding us welcome to a Baptist
Church on wheels, but no pews these aisles bestrewn with countless
layers of putrid wastes
beneath a vast bulging complement of animals (caged
and uncaged, alike), livestock, fowl,
barnyard creatures
in all sizes malodorous: underfed, scrawny goats,
diarrheal lambs trying to nurse from ailing mother sheep
tucked under old farmlady's seat, its dugs dried up, oozing serums
where the disgruntled litter had lacerated her flesh,
pustulate from infections blent with fetid streams issuing from babes

with the runs: toddler humans   ,
squalling on laps, or worse, plotzed on the aisle
floor, awash in beast swamp pools . . .

          2

    "Why the devil," I growl at the driver
       beside me, "must we keep recircling this maze
       of inner-city Jacmel rounds, when it's obvious the van
    is full to capacity, and beyond?" He ignores my feeble harassment,
       even when my voice is raised to match, or exceed,
    his own strident volley of threats aimed, by turns, at the succession
  of outdoors hitchhikers
dangled from the sides, one arm hooked over a window,
    the other grasping some unseen rail
       in the baggage racks:
          amazingly, they all maintain their footing
          on the narrow splintered running boards which rim
       the bus's exterior bottom edge, despite frequent lunges into potholes
          which feel severe enough to snap an axle, the shocks
       worn so low; those bus undersides not much raised above the roadway,
    our cabin floor itself
seems battered directly upon rocks and road gravel,
    the worst knocks transmitted, nakedly,

          through warped floorboards
       to our foot soles. I must check my sneakers,
    at intervals, to be reminded
       a floor survives at all, absorbing some of the blows
          which seem to strike my feet unmediated, as if my shoes,
             fallen through punctures
                in the flooring, are dragged across road
          surface . . . Now rising in his seat, the driver vindictively howls
             at several bus-flank

hitchers who ride three-deep, two small men
    piled on the back and shoulders of a husky bloke
    who grips the window frame. Evidently, he's paid his tip,
or nominal hitch-a-ride pittance, but that scant fee doesn't include
    an extra team of passengers heaped-up piggyback
    behind him, which generates a fierce dialogue of cusswords and alibis,
both disputants chattering
at once; neither pauses, whether to listen or catch
    breath, an adversarial style each
        accepts as *a given:*
            the status quo an unavoidable nonstop talk void
            between them, which grows more heated, until freeloaders
jump off at their destinations, or pay a few extra farthings, smokes,
    or fruit. All such side-hanger tagalong rides
are illegal and punishable by large fines, I've heard; both driver
    and hitcher, if caught,
face jail terms, as well. But the law's never enforced,
    since most van cabbies rake in

        half again more cash
    from the hop-on, hop-off squadrons than revenues
earned from ticketed indoors occupants,
    a high percentage graft skimmed off the top each week
        to muzzle road marshals who patrol the bus route beats.
        Though faces of side-hitcher
            parasites keep changing, while luggage packs
are added and removed, amid shrieks and curses, I know we circuit,
    bizarrely, the same frenzied

    trial run, repeated many times over.
        What circle in *The Inferno,* I wonder, may befit
        and house this never-ending treadmill, which resembles,
    more and more, a hell with no exits; I myself a Carib Trotter Faust,
        while our driver is close exemplar of Creole

Mephistopheles: our bargain struck, the journey's fee is paid in advance,
　no way to interrupt
the Mephisto Waltz I've begun, or break the endless
　cycle. This sad *early* bus grows
　　late, ever later,
　　　dashing our hopes for prompt return to our villa
　　　in the Capital. We're stuck in a turnstile that spins
　　one way only, so there's no turning back. And now, we've been stalled
　　　for the third time at Jacmel's most popular
　　flophouse speakeasy. I hold up three fingers to the mad chauffeur
　of our whirligig course,
and plead: "*Trois, trois,* it's time to hit the countryside.
Why, O why, do we keep coming back

　　to this funky hostel?
　Same place, three stops before!" "*Oui, oui,*" he says.
"We're full to safety capacity seating,
　but the Law requires scheduled stops at all public houses,
　　lodgings, inns, for pickup or delivery of all shipped goods."
　　　Those cargoes, I've noted,
　　　are either mountainously piled and strapped
　to roof-rack carriers, or squeezed into those deep-shelved bins tucked
　　under the rear floor frames.

　　"Emergency late arrival," he declares,
　　　while handymen above lower a huge wooden crate,
　　　a contraption of wheels and pulleys, upon the swelled roof—
　　just over our heads—from the third story of the flophouse, followed
　　　by a vast animal cage, clunkily dropped and shaken,
　　the enraged quadrupeds letting loose a cantata of squawks, heehaws
　and bleats . . . Or so, my ear
deciphers that immiscible blend of creaturely sounds;
　indeed, who can guess which of the Lord's
　　most incompatible

brutes and genial nuzzlers have been cramped
　　　　into the one dank crib for pained upper-deck transport?
　　Next, glancing in the driver seat side mirror, I espy several honchos
　　　　(three Mr. Universe pectoral- and bicep-enlarged
　　types), slowly letting down the airborne zoo: a feather-bespattering,
snout-poky, hoof-kicking,
white-nub-of-tail-stubble wagging between the bars wriggly
　　great cage! Noah's ark in the sky

　　　　bobbled on our roof,
　　we keep having to edge forward a few inches,
then back, to delicately fit the huge box
　　　into the rooftop unseen mosaic of crates, satchels, bins,
　　　　cages, bushel baskets . . . The art of stacking so diversified
　　　　a misfit of cable-bound,
　　　　　　or rope-tied and taped and stapled packages,
　　adroitly, on a single vehicular two-story-high roof, I've observed
　　　is no small feat.

Swimming Pool Pastoral

All bags parked
and shelved in our snug bungalow,
we stroll toward the beach—both sorry antique
Hotel Barrymore
(famous old noble house converted
in the midfifties)
is so far from shore. We hug the fence,
most cattle and goats grazing on the far side, for now;
but missing fence segments let barnyard
fowl and heifers wander
freely through Inn grounds, between cottages,
across open courtyard. Puzzled
by such laxities

in a posh setting,
we tarry: scan dark storm clouds
thickening overhead, late afternoon drizzle
just begun. Downpour
imminent. Turntail, we reverse
our course, hurry back
to the Inn—you all disappointment,
trailing a net bag, bulging with masks, snorkels, flippers.
You don this gear, a skindiver's
full accoutrements,
and sweep across the Barrymore swimming pool's
length, many underwater laps
swiftly rocketed—

too near ceramic
floor? From above, you appear
to scrape bottom with your shoulders, knees
(the lowest *keel* parts
of you), making a to-and-fro pool
circuit twice before once

coming up for air. Oh happy gymnast
blessed with nonsmoker's surplus lung spans, you hoard
the whole pool to yourself an hour
in heaviest rains
chopping the surface, corrugating the hides
of reflected cow and goats—
oddly mirrored

on the pool face—
trotting past, while the head maid
shoos the snorting interlopers with a broom,
percussive hooves
tapping on slippery floor tiles . . .
I gasp! A tilted ox
may shamble sideways into the pool
and trample your sleek, flaxen head, blond neck, blond back,
like so much loose straw aswirl
traversing the blurred
pool bottom—the brute in such a blind panic
to escape the whisks and blows
of irate hostess.

But you porpoise
upward at the pool's near end,
the propulsion of your spring so strong I expect
you to collide
with the diving board's underside:
you scramble in midair,
those flippered feet—like a figure skater's
rubbery ice skates—twisting about, odd mask and snorkel
giving your head a gargoyle's
acromegalic profile.
You snap up a black box, unnoticed at poolside,

which I don't recognize as Kodak
Instamatic until,

thin strap twisted
over one shoulder and under chin,
you flash quick shots of the stalled livestock.
Vertiginous cow
and goats, struggling to maneuver
swiftly in the cramped space
between pool and bar, devise a frantic
circling trot, their raised hooves crisscrossing each other
as they shimmy and shuffle—
queer round dance
step, while you converge on their wavery haunches
for close-ups. Suddenly, cow back-trots!
You dodge, just before

she'd have pancaked
you sideways into the patio wall.
Only now do you hear—much less heed!—my reproof
to give wide berth
for those perilous rear hooves, *cudgels,*
sliding and pummeling
tile mosaic, by turns, some ten or twenty
brilliant-colored patio tiles shattered by their impact.
Oh, think of equivalent damages
to fragile small bones
in your feet, or frailer toes, I say, tugging
you back by one shoulder, and clear
of the adjacent cow's

wriggly orbit. I'd
be helpless to budge your sinewy,
agile frame if not for the superior traction

of my sneakers' soles
on wet tiles, as against your bare feet
(in the prance and tumult,
you've kicked off flippers) . . . What now! Pool
jumps, leaps from its sunken confines: whole watery mass
flying skyward, all-of-a-piece, it seems,
before my incredulous
eye—refusing the absurd sight—records images
of a vast obesity of blubber,
or lard, fallen

from its pedestal,
four lamppost-skinny legs. The ox
colossus, expanding as it drops, strange hooves
kicking at the upwards-
falling pool water, lands on its back . . .
My slow brain tries
to use simple math to cope with tradeoff,
or visual reversal: the heifer's bulk and the pool's
change places, trade *below* and *above,*
rawhide sack-of-beef
units volume equals so many liquid units
cubic volume; not to say the one
six-letter verb

which best expresses
the freakish displacement of liquid
and solid bodies in air—SPLASH . . . The upflung
hulk of water shrinks
in space, above, while the head-over-heels
belly-up beast expands
below, seems to double or triple in size,
inflating like a blowfish before my eyes: the huge butt—
rump and hindquarters—striking bottom,

at pool's shallow end,
　　with a heavy muffled thud: seismic rumbles,
the whole surrounding patio shaken.
　　　　One bounce. Sounds

　　　　of bone, or glazed tile,
cracking. Softer thuds. Oafish bovinity
　　twisted onto its side, now, some water returned,
　　　　perhaps cushioning
the shock and succession of aftershocks,
as the pained quadruped,
　　half-crippled, struggles to raise itself
from a cavity in the pool floor gouged by its falls.
At a safe remove and vantage, ourselves,
　　beyond pool's deep end
　　　　(diving board looking queerly naked and high-
risen over the shrunk contents),
　　　　I catch glimpses

　　　　of five barstool
squatters, flying off at all angles:
　　an instant rodeo, riders ditch their saddles—
　　　　foam seats turned bronco—
to evade the deluge of tidal wave's
unstoppable advance.
　　Two tipsy lads leap over the high bar,
vanishing on the bottle side; a third stretched out
lengthwise, belly-down on the bar top,
　　letting fly glassware
　　　　shrapnel six ways; while the buxom mahogany-
faced barmaid ducks through wall
　　　　panel escape hatch . . .

These manifold
events, sorted into starkly etched
blocks in space and italicized by my eyes'
speed-of-light notation,
erupted simultaneously: a *diorama,*
no more than three seconds
spanning the total spectrum of man-beast
dislocations. *So it is, the Eye, with careless genius,*
condenses and transcribes the World's
Cyclotron Flux
of data. No forced slowdown of words, voiced
breaths . . . But talk comes fast, now,
our jabber blurted

in the backwash
and aftermath of pool's dissolution,
while we await the arrival of Paramedic Squad
and All-Island Swat Team,
summoned by the Barrymore's manager
to fetch rescue gear:
an ingenious contraption of chains, hooks,
and motor-driven pulleys, chug-chugging, which extracts
the deadweight of lame bovine sludge
deposit flattened
to the drained pool shell (cow the sole casualty,
we muse, all Pulmotor resuscitation
efforts failed) . . .

LAURENCE LIEBERMAN's work has been widely anthologized; his poems and critical essays have appeared in most of the country's leading magazines—*The New Yorker, The American Poetry Review, The Hudson Review, New England Review, The Kenyon Review,* and *Sewanee Review* among them. He is the author of six previous books of poetry—*The Creole Mephistopheles* (1989), *The Mural of Wakeful Sleep* (1985), *Eros at the World Kite Pageant* (1983), *God's Measurements* (1980), *The Osprey Suicides* (1973), and *The Unblinding* (1968)—as well as a collection of essays on contemporary American poets, *Unassigned Frequencies: American Poetry in Review* (1977). Lieberman received the Jerome Shestack Prize from *The American Poetry Review* for the title sequence from *The Mural of Wakeful Sleep,* and he won a Creative Writing Fellowship in poetry from the National Endowment for the Arts, supporting his cycle of Caribbean poetry books in progress. A Professor of English at the University of Illinois, he has received three appointments as Associate in the Center for Advanced Study, and was awarded an Arnold Beckman Fellowship in Fall 1993.

Illinois Poetry Series
Laurence Lieberman, Editor

Moon in a Mason Jar
Robert Wrigley (1986)

Lower-Class Heresy
T. R. Hummer (1987)

Poems: New and Selected
Frederick Morgan (1987)

Furnace Harbor: A Rhapsody of the
North Country
Philip D. Church (1988)

Bad Girl, with Hawk
Nance Van Winckel (1988)

Blue Tango
Michael Van Walleghen (1989)

Eden
Dennis Schmitz (1989)

Waiting for Poppa at the Smithtown
Diner
Peter Serchuk (1990)

Great Blue
Brendan Galvin (1990)

What My Father Believed
Robert Wrigley (1991)

Something Grazes Our Hair
S. J. Marks (1991)

Walking the Blind Dog
G. E. Murray (1992)

The Sawdust War
Jim Barnes (1992)

The God of Indeterminacy
Sandra McPherson (1993)

National Poetry Series

Eroding Witness
Nathaniel Mackey (1985)
Selected by Michael Harper

Palladium
Alice Fulton (1986)
Selected by Mark Strand

Cities in Motion
Sylvia Moss (1987)
Selected by Derek Walcott

The Hand of God and a Few Bright
Flowers
William Olsen (1988)
Selected by David Wagoner

The Great Bird of Love
Paul Zimmer (1989)
Selected by William Stafford

Stubborn
Roland Flint (1990)
Selected by Dave Smith

The Surface
Laura Mullen (1991)
Selected by C. K. Williams

The Dig
Lynn Emanuel (1992)
Selected by Gerald Stern

My Alexandria
Mark Doty (1993)
Selected by Philip Levine

Other Poetry Volumes

Her Soul beneath the Bone: Women's
Poetry on Breast Cancer
Edited by Leatrice Lifshitz (1988)

Days from a Dream Almanac
Dennis Tedlock (1990)

Working Classics: Poems on Industrial
Life
*Edited by Peter Oresick and Nicholas
Coles* (1990)

Hummers, Knucklers, and Slow Curves:
Contemporary Baseball Poems
Edited by Don Johnson (1991)

The Double Reckoning of Christopher
Columbus
Barbara Helfgott Hyett (1992)

Selected Poems
Jean Garrigue (1992)

New and Selected Poems, 1962–92
Laurence Lieberman (1993)

Why did you stay away from minimalist poetry?
What do you feel your place in society as a poet is?
Do you think poetry is bred by & for colleges?
Do you think there will ever be a shift back toward
    classical forms?

Personal & instinctively charged ~~crit~~ critical essays.

What role do the forms you create play for you as writer
    What are they meant to do for a reader?

Why longer poems? → do you feel writing is a task or a calling

Do ever feel a reserve about people that you know & that are alive.

Says William Stafford put writing above the poem itself,
Stafford looks for the moment... The intuative moment was important
instead of the crafted piece. He